Baptism by Fire

Bantam Books

New York   Toronto   London
Sydney   Auckland

Baptism by Fire

The true story of a mother

who finds faith

during her daughter's

darkest hour

Heather Choate Davis

BAPTISM BY FIRE
A Bantam Book / February 1998

The excerpt from the poem "Your children are not your children . . . ,"
from *The Prophet* by Kahlil Gibran, copyright 1923 by Kahlil Gibran and
renewed 1951 by Administrators CTA of Kahlil Gibran Estate and Mary
G. Gibran, is reprinted by permission of Alfred A. Knopf, Inc.

Library of Congress Cataloging-in-Publication Data

Davis, Heather Choate.
  Baptism by fire : a true story of a mother who finds faith during her
  daughter's darkest hour / Heather Choate Davis,
        p.   cm.
  ISBN 0-553-10645-7 (hardcover)
  1. Davis, Heather Choate.   2. Christian biography—United States.
  3. Mothers and daughters—United States.   I. Title.
  BR1725.D365A3   1998
  277.3'082—dc21
  [B]   97-31704
                                                            CIP

Published simultaneously in the United States and Canada

Bantam Books are published by Bantam Books, a division of Bantam
Doubleday Dell Publishing Group, Inc. Its trademark, consisting of the
words "Bantam Books" and the portrayal of a rooster, is Registered in U.S.
Patent and Trademark Office and in other countries. Marca Registrada.
Bantam Books, 1540 Broadway, New York, New York 10036.

Printed in the United States of America
BVG   10   9   8   7   6   5   4   3   2   1

To Graham, who led the way.

brunch, where I would give thanks for the honeydew and the raspberries, the custard-oozing éclairs, the steaming stainless troughs of bacon and sausage and the perfectly browned triangles of warm French toast.

As I neared adolescence I was enrolled for confirmation classes. I attended the first one, skipped the next eight, and popped back in on the very last day asking to take the entire course load of makeup exams and the final. The instructor walked me down a long corridor to a private room. "Take your time, dear, take your time," he said telegraphically, then closed the door and left me alone with a stack of Bibles and fourteen pages of fill-in-the-passage questions. It was no great stretch from there to here: If religion was meant to be taken seriously, they would have declined to confirm me. They would have stood their ground and said, "We look forward to having you join us for the complete ten-session course next semester."

Instead, I took my place in my new butter-yellow Saks Fifth Avenue dress knowing that I had cheated wholeheartedly and with seeming permission on my confirmation exam. The whole congregation smiled and cheered and people I had never met slipped little envelopes in my hand. This ceremony was to mark my first conscious and informed steps closer to god, but I don't remember any discussion of that. There was, however, a great deal of talk about how The Club had started featuring made-to-order omelettes with the fillings of your choice, a safe and pleasant topic to carry us through the back roads of Beverly Hills and on into the dining hall, which on that day, as on all Sundays, was upholstered with monarchies of hard-boned, well-powdered widows, strapping, tie-clipped men, broochey, sexless wives and the clamor of seersuckered IIs and IIIs.

The maître d' sat us at a small table overlooking the 18th hole. We had hardly unfolded the starched green napkins when my mom, with her free-swinging hair and unmatronly skirt, shook her head and observed, as if for the first time, "I just can't believe this place still doesn't have any black people."

"Oh, for goodness' sake, Mary, what are you talking about? We only hire black people," my grandmother replied, ripping open her blueberry muffin with an ice-hard pat of butter.

With that my dad rose. "Well, if one of them ever comes around," he said, pulling out my chair, "order me a Bloody Mary, would you? A double, hold the celery." He smiled down on me with his game-show-host grin. "C'mon, princess, let's go get a plate."

In honor of my big day, my dad had given me a fourteen-karat-gold bracelet engraved with my name. It was the first real jewelry I ever had. As we walked toward the buffet, my wrist swinging back and forth in his tan, manicured hand, the gold caught the light with such taunting brilliance that I could not look away, and I was certain that I, so adored and so sparkly, was the envy of The Club.

I was my father's daughter. I had his dark eyes and his Roman nose, his quick mind, his penchant for word games and his boundless, driving ambition. I had always adored being told I was just like him, until his drinking turned from a curious stash of Clorets in the glove compartment of his Jaguar to an eight-year battle with cirrhosis played out in a variety of hospital beds and drunken theatrics.

He had a romantic's love of New England. It had been his dream for me to go to college there, but, after a year of elaborate planning, he became mysteriously unavailable for our much ballyhooed, father-daughter East Coast college junket just days before. "Your father's not going to be able to take you, sweetie," my mom relayed to me gently. I flashed for a moment on my solid gold confirmation bracelet and how it had turned my wrist green. "Okay, that's okay," I said, as I had said many times before. I could fix it. I went straight to my yellow pad—the tool he had taught me so well to rely on—and began recouping the plan with my mom in his stead.

I graduated from high school three weeks after my seventeenth birthday and starting packing my footlocker the next day. I had chosen Northeastern University in Boston, because of their cooperative work-study program. I had no intention of staying in school the full four years. I had plans, big plans. I had spent my formative years with *Bewitched*'s Darrin Stephens and Mr. Tate and was quite certain that I was going to do what they did although, at the time, I had no idea what that particular job was called. "Advertising," I'd say. "The word part, not the art part."

A month after I moved away, I got a call that my father had fallen naked from the roof of his three-story apartment building in Marina del Rey. It was two o'clock in the afternoon. He told the doctors that the reason he had been standing on the ledge of the rooftop was that god was trying to talk to him and he wanted to hear what he had to say, but I found his explanation highly suspect. He had taken as much pride in his atheism as he had in his alibis.

All told, I flew cross-country five times to say good-bye to my father, to sit by his hospital bedside for weeks at a stretch and wait for him to die, but he would not. He hung on despite all medical wisdom as his liver rotted and his veins ruptured and he coughed up blood made unmanageable by vodka. On my twenty-first birthday, I called my dad from a kitchen in suburban Ohio where I was a reluctant houseguest. My boyfriend, an alcoholic–coke addict eleven years my senior, had just gotten out of rehab and wanted me with him as he leeched emotional support from his seventy-five-year-old father, his father's prim young wife and their three gangly kids. My birthday celebration consisted of fish sticks and ambrosia on TV trays in an airless sunroom with five wholesome strangers and a man who later that night would sneak out of our bed to chug a bottle of NyQuil. "Excuse me," I said, slipping into the kitchen; I didn't want to cry in front of them. I wanted to be alone to call my dad and hear him say, "Happy birthday, princess," but he had no idea who I was.

Later that year, I was lured back home by a large L.A. advertising agency. There, I would meet Lon. He reminded me of the ocean, of the plunge of deep waves, of salt, of strong currents. There was not a shiny, hard-edged thing about him. He had a wordless sensuality that I dismissed at

5

first as heat, but then it washed over me like seafoam, settling low and smooth, a feeling of peace, a calm that nestled in my belly and poured over my chest without fanfare or drama, proclaiming in the softest of voices, *I am here now.* Our first Christmas together he gave me an airbrushed painting he had done years before. It was of a middle-aged couple in swimsuits at the beach. The sky is black. The man is planted deep in the sand in a mesh-weave beach chair and he is turned away, watching her—not her long back, not her soft hips, but her raptus, which on this particular day has driven her to point a camera straight into the white-hot glare of a solar eclipse.

The first time Lon came with me to the hospital, it was to ask for my hand—a gesture, really, since we'd been planning the wedding for months. My father was particularly lucid that day, telling Lon that I "was the most important thing in the world" and making him promise to take good care of me. Lon said, "I'll water her regularly and make sure she gets plenty of sun." My dad grinned in a way I hadn't seen in years, and died two days later.

The memorial service was so sparsely attended that we decided at the last minute to move into a tiny alcove chapel off the main church; even then, the postage stamp of rowed chairs went unfilled. The rector did what she could to honor the life of a man she'd never met, but her words could not hold my attention. I was drawn to the glint of an old gold font, realizing in that moment that he had stood there once, my father, nattily dressed and gleaming, smug, his daughter wrapped snugly in his arms. My stomach collapsed to the womb. My veins surged so effusively that I could scarcely breathe. I pressed my head against Lon's shoulder and sought to comfort myself with the nihilistic shrug I'd picked up from my drug-addict boyfriend: "Life's a funny old dog."

2.

seeing things

Graham came into our lives after four years of marriage and eight hours of unmedicated labor. I remember looking at Lon as the head was crowning. Despite the fact that he had read every book, attended every class, breathed every breath with me, it was as if just then—just in that instant—the pregnancy was hitting him in a physical way. "This is a really big deal," he said, and turned ashen. And then we were three.

Hours blurred, defined by little else than the need for food or sleep. *"I love you, sweet angel,"* I purred, asking nothing in return. *"I love you,"* I sang again and again, infusing Graham with every ounce of my being, liquid or otherwise, from dawn to dusk and back again. "*I love you,*" I said, and waited. Just as the scourge of sleepless nights threatened to end the honeymoon, it came, his small, wet mouth curling up at both corners and igniting the universe. The ecstasy of men and women pales in comparison. In the evening, it was Lon's gentle hand that would smooth liquid suds into each nook and fold of our son—*thank you,* he would say, but not in words, *this is everything,* he would whisper, but not aloud—as his deep blue eyes pierced mine through the eye of the video camera and foretold new ecstasies for us too.

Words came quickly to Graham, one after another, then in chunks and strings and ceaseless curiosities. Our explorations stacked and spawned like Tinkertoys as he devoured the world and I devoted myself to his seeing it in all its shades. I didn't have much patience for cutting crusts off of sandwiches or the endless tying of shoes, but I would drop anything to show him how a pot of water comes to a boil, how pollen relocates, airplanes rise, colors blend or nutmeg tastes; that piano keys can sound happy or sad; that a gardener with a leaf blower in a windstorm is worth wondering about. One day when he was a toddler we happened upon this: There, in front of our neighborhood fire station, was an engine ladder pointing straight up into the sky. It wasn't leaning on or toward anything at all, but stretched three stories high in a near-perfect vertical like a metaphor against a backdrop of pale, unobstructed blue—thirty stainless steps like a back entrance to heaven. I parked the van. We approached the veteran firefighter positioned next to the base of the truck to inquire. "Yeah, well, it's cleanup time—we do this twice a year. Extend them all the way, wash out the cracks, make sure everything is—"

"Oh my god," I shouted, suddenly spotting Graham well atop the engine's raised platform. On every previous visit, it had taken several minutes just to coax him into the driver's seat.

"Graham," I said, hurdling the back bumper to climb on board.

"I'll get him," the fireman said, and leapt up to the base of the ladder. Graham had already started to climb it. He was not a big climber, and he never tried something new without looking back at me first, if not for permission, then to make sure I was watching. But on this day, up he went, four rungs, five, not looking down. Not looking back at me. The firefighter stood planted at the base of the ladder, watching. "How old is he?" he asked in disbelief.

"He's not even two," I said as he worked his way up, nine rungs, ten.

"I've never seen anything like it," he said. "We have field trips here all the time, but I've never—"

He continued on, twelve rungs, thirteen. My eyes drifted sideways to a reference point—a streetlight. Graham was looking down on it. "Aren't you going to get him?"

The firefighter stepped up two rungs. "I'm right behind him. I'd like to see what he's going to do—this is unbelievable." It felt for a moment like Graham might climb straight up through the clouds and never come back. I watched, head back, mouth open like a breath postponed, awestricken but surprisingly unafraid. Somehow it seemed like he belonged up there in the sky.

"Look, Mom, I'm almost there," he said, four rungs from the top. When he turned around to look for me, he started to wobble. My hands shot like a reflex over my face, fingers touching like a tent. Like a prayer.

"All right, buddy, I think we better come on down now," the firefighter said calmly, and scooped him up without missing a beat.

The whole way home I watched my son out of the corner of my eye. "The fireman said he'd never seen anything like it," I said. Graham smiled the most self-satisfied smile and looked out the window, thinking—what, I will never know.

I rarely remember my dreams, but there are three that now stick with me. The first one occurred a month after my brother Michael's telling chest X ray, and just after I drove my car full speed into the center divider of the San Diego Freeway. Graham was nearly two.

I was in the ocean, very deep down. It was very black and very cold but I kept submerging, deeper, farther down, pushing the water away with my hands, searching, descending. Suddenly, I happened upon a couple. It was Graham's godfather, Rob, and his new fiancée. I had introduced them—in real life—that spring and they had fallen in love instantly, filling their days with secret notes and shopping sprees and their nights with slow, elegant dinners and playfulness. They were engaged three months later. In my dream they were standing by the sink doing their dishes in a circle of pure light, and I looked at them, confused. "Why don't you have any lamps around here?" I asked them. "Oh, we don't need any," they said. "But where is it? Where is the light coming from?" I pleaded, and in perfect unison, they turned their heads and looked up. The image seemed to zoom through the dark, murky water and up through the sky, focusing our attention on the moon, which spun around several times, then came to a stop. "There will be light," they said, and smiled. "There will be light again."

Graham was four by the time I felt brave enough to commit to a second child. Lon wanted a daughter, desperately. He would say again and again that whatever we had would be just fine, but nonetheless I knew. I had been a daughter. This time around I would be the mother; this time around I would be on the receiving end. Over the next nine months I was often heard to say, "If it's a boy, I'll be relieved."

At ten weeks I started to bleed. It stopped for a bit, then started again, stopped, then started, heavier than before. This went on for days and into a long, dark Saturday night when we were expected at a big outdoor birthday bash thrown in Rob's honor by his new bride. Old friends circled round with sparklers and champagne to congratulate me on the joyous news; I nodded and sputtered and fled to the bathroom, crouching over my warm, anxious body, certain that I would miscarry while a growing line of party-goers stood knocking on the bathroom door. *Please, no, not my little girl,* I pleaded; to whom, I couldn't say. I became somber, resigned. We went home early and I lay in bed anguishing . . . *don't take her from me, I beg of you* . . . and fell into a deep sleep.

In the morning the bleeding had stopped. My doctor ordered an ultrasound to check the placenta, and all appeared to be perfect. I discussed my pregnancy guardedly for the next few weeks, but time passed and lo and behold I was fourteen weeks pregnant, with a small pooch and the last wave of nausea behind me.

"Oh, it's definitely a girl," friends became fond of saying. "She's already giving you a hard time."

I didn't like that particular sentiment. I can remember my mom saying on more than one occasion that my 4′ 10″ grand-mother was sent to bed for the full term of her gestation and had hated her ever since. But secretly, I liked hearing these predictions of a daughter—however groundless—spoken with such confidence.

Gamine colt unfurled
under gray and heavy skies
A thunderous entrance, yours.
February 4, 1994

My second child was due on Valentine's Day. Lon had gotten me the soundtrack to the movie *The Piano* for Christ-mas and every morning I would play it quite loudly, won-dering, as the haunting melody reverberated through the house, if it was as disturbing to her as it was to me. Would she, as a result, be born stormy and melancholy? Brooding and mute? If I ever took a lover, would she hide under my bedroom window, as the young girl in the movie had done, and watch? Would she let Lon chop off my finger, then run gleefully through a field gripping it in a bloody rag to deliver as a warning? Of course she would, I decided as I brushed the crumbs from the shelf below my breasts. That's what little girls do for their daddies. That's what little girls do to their mommies.

While February dragged its fat heels, I had the second dream. It was a girl. I could see her deep blue eyes and her endlessly long legs. I could feel her warm, slippery body emerging from mine, and I could speak to her as a teenager. She was magnificent. I awakened to stormy skies and felt compelled to write a poem—a haiku—but then lost control of the form and let the words spread out. My womb cramped and spasmed. I was certain I was documenting the moments immediately preceding her birth, but she was not ready, and I was left to lumber on, lugging my dark thoughts and my elephantine belly up and down the Venice canals.

"Want to know what that is?" a gray-haired man baited me in passing.

"Won't know for a few more days," I said with a curt smile.

"Oh, don't have to wait a few more days. I'll tell you right now. That's a boy."

"Are you a doctor?" I inquired, holding my face in an unnaturally placating expression.

"No, but I just know. I can tell. That's a boy if ever I've seen one."

"I don't know . . . ," I said, mock smile held firmly. "We'll see."

"Nothing to see—that's a boy, sure as I'm standing here. Good luck to you."

I waddled over the bridge, gouging a path through the milling of neighborhood ducks. My friend Lynne lived just around the corner. We had raised our first kids together and she and her husband, Greg, were to be this child's godparents.

"I am so sick of people coming up to me saying, 'It's a boy. It's a boy.' That whole thing about how you're carrying is bullshit. I mean, it doesn't make any sense. Why would what you're carrying affect your body shape? It's ridiculous. You carry the way you carry. It's based on body type. This is just how I carry—period. If one more person comes up and says, 'Oh, that's a boy,' I'm going to scream!"

"But you don't want a girl, right?" said Lynne, bemused.

"No, I don't. I don't care. I mean, it's not like I get any say in it anyway. I just don't want people to keep saying it's a boy, that's all. It pisses me off!"

"It's okay to want a girl."

"I don't. I'm not into all that girl stuff—those ridiculous lace headbands and those candy-flavored makeup kits and all those silly shoes. I don't want to drape my kid in plastic beads and teach her to shrug her shoulders. I'm just not into the whole thing."

"Uh-huh," she said, biting her tongue and wiping yogurt

off her younger daughter's face. "Well, whatever it is as long as it's healthy."

"Of course, right," I replied. "Whatever it is as long as it's healthy."

The contractions started on a Sunday afternoon. By the time we arrived at the hospital, I was five centimeters dilated and rapidly transitioning. I lay on my side and panted hard in Lon's face; there was no letup, no break, no pause long enough to discuss medication. I breathed hard, wailed loudly, and my childhood girlfriend Christine dutifully pressed a tennis ball into my back for fifty-six minutes. The doctor on call arrived, broke my membranes and said, "You can push whenever you want," but I wasn't sure I wanted to. It was even more painful than I remembered. This kid was big. Eleven minutes later I made the final push. They lifted the baby to my chest. I groped desperately at the warm, slippery form and thought I was going to drop it.

"It's a girl," they echoed.

"It's a girl? We have a girl. Oh my god, Lon, it's a girl," I wept, and Lon double-checked. She weighed in at an abundantly healthy nine pounds, five ounces and measured a leggy twenty-one and a half inches. She was perfect. Exquisite. Our daughter, Remy Choate Davis. I can remember then a feeling that I know will stay with me for the rest of my life, a feeling greater even than my wedding day or the birth of my firstborn . . . *I have a daughter. I have a boy and a girl and we're done. How did I get so lucky?*

She was born at 9:16 P.M. and we were home by dinnertime the next night. The Winter Olympics had just begun and

16

Remy and I sat up late into the night nursing and cheering. She was at my breast when Dan Jansen faltered once again in his strongest event, leaving the entire flag-waving, TV-watching, god-revering world at a loss. He had worked so hard, he had suffered so much, he had forged ahead with dignity and faith, and everything we knew in the core of our beings told us that this time—this Olympics—he was entitled to his gold medal. It had to be. We needed proof that god played fair. And so it was the next day, in a race that was not his forte, he would have his long-awaited win. As he took his starlit victory lap with his baby girl held tight in his arms, the relief was palpable; the world let out its collective breath and wept its collective tears. I cradled Remy in kind, and somehow all was as it should be once more—safe, snug, bleary-eyed, but complete.

How did I get so lucky?

I have often heard that when something violent or fatal happens to a child the mother knows instantly; she startles from a deep sleep or is overcome with some preternatural awareness of events. I'd had no personal experience with this, but I believed it to be true. Premonitions, on the other hand, seemed less reliable. Not that I didn't believe there were certain occasional glimmers from some larger picture; I just didn't understand how a person could be trusted to cull the psychic from the merely worrisome.

When it came, this insistent image, it was like a scene from a drive-in movie hot-wired into my frontal lobe. It appeared to me like this: *There is a boot. A large, black, pointy boot. Then Remy. Then the boot enters the frame with Remy's angelic face*

17

and bashes in her left temple. There is a strident, horrific music cue like the one that accompanies Sissy Spacek's whiplike head turns as she slams the auditorium doors shut in the climactic prom scene of the movie Carrie. *And then, in a heartbeat, it's gone.*

There was no rhyme or reason to it. It was not like when a parent sees a ceiling fan and an infant in the same room and can't help but imagine the infant being lifted up lovingly and decapitated; there was no one wearing boots in our home. The timing of the vision was very specific. Remy and I were on the couch, nursing, bonding, when suddenly I was flooded with a surge of love that spread across my heart like warm syrup on pancakes and I felt at long last what it was for me to love a daughter. *We would read* Little Women *together. We would read* Little House on the Prairie *and* Pippi Longstocking *and watch gymnastics on TV.* This was the moment when the boot first struck.

After that, the identical vision—the boot, her head, the savage kick to the left temple, the screeching jolt of instantaneous sound and movement—came steadfast and unrelenting, assaulting our quietest moments at least once a week till Remy was seven and a half months old. Having no idea what to make of it, I dismissed it as hormones or exhaustion or something like fear.

3.

the tree of death

They found my mom's breast cancer right after Graham was born. I can remember sitting on the couch, my infant son sucking at me ravenously, and feeling certain that it was I who was going to die. Suddenly, there was a flaw in my previously flawless genetic heritage. A bad gene. A loose cannon. A "yes" box that would now have to be checked on a medical history. I was forced to dip one toe into the dark pool of *them*. Them the cursed. Them the damned. Them the sick ones. The unlucky ones. The ones who don't take care of themselves.

I drove her to the oncologist's. I heard about the statistics, and the surgery, and the chemo that would follow. I heard about lumpectomies and mastectomies and lymph nodes. I heard about how—she being nearly menopausal—her breast cancer did not affect heredity the way it would if she had gotten it in her thirties.

"Well, I'm only twenty-eight, and I've already given birth once. And I'm breastfeeding exclusively," I said, as if the only possible response to that would be *"Oh well, in that case, I wouldn't give it a second thought."*

"I know that those circumstances have been fairly widely reported in the media as decreasing the risks, but in truth—in my experience—I have never found a correlation there great enough to hang your hat on," the oncologist said dryly.

I was there when the anesthesia wore off, but my visit was short. I had read somewhere that a loving husband should ask to see the place where the breast had been cut away. It did not say what daughters were supposed to do. Over the course of my life I had been her watchdog, her confidante, her advisor and her best friend. But I was not her husband, and I did not want to see it. I had a newborn at home, a son whose need for me was so primeval that a passing baby in the hall shot milk through my chest like a hurled arrow.

"I'm not sure if I can come back tomorrow. It's hard to be away from the baby this long," I said, leaning over her awkwardly, my engorged breasts pressing against her bandages. "I'll call you." I was almost to the elevator when I heard a voice from behind.

"Hey," he said.

I turned to find my brother, Michael. My mom often said that people thought he was handsome, but I didn't see it. I just saw the edginess, the beads of discomfort rising up through his pale, flushed skin, the effort to be casual that could, on a dime, turn vicious.

"Hey, I hear you're a mom now," he chirped, leaning in for a kiss. We had not seen each other since my father's funeral five years before. Even then, we had not spoken. "Wow, that's great. It's a boy, right? You've got a boy," he continued, standing too close. I used the contact to assess his breath.

"Yes, a boy," I said, and stepped over to the elevator button.

"Graham, right? His name is Graham? Boy, I can't believe I'm an uncle. Can you believe it? Uncle Mike. Has a nice ring to it, don't you think?"

"Listen, I've got to get home—"

"You got any pictures?"

"What?"

"Pictures. Of my nephew?"

"No," I said, the words like a mist, "not on me," I continued, turning my head away toward the down button. "Why don't you go in and keep Mom company? I'm sure she'll be glad to see you."

"Mom already showed me a bunch of pictures. She gave me one for my wallet."

I pushed the button three times hard without turning around. "Well, then you've seen him."

Michael flashed a victorious grin as I turned away once and for all. "Hey, Heath," he said, like a blowtorch at my back.

"Good-bye, Michael."

"Don't fuck him up."

The specter of my brother was a powerful incentive to be a hands-on parent. Stay home with the kids, give them everything you've got, then, if they turn out wretched and want to blame it all on you, you'll be able to slam the door with a clear conscience. My mother's blind and crippling support of her abusive adult son made me suspect that her conscience was not clear.

"It's different this time," my mother said a year after her surgery; a year cancer free. "He's been sober for nine months now."

"Sober nine months for what, the tenth time?" I responded.

"He really wants to meet his nephew. He wants to be a part of his life. Will you please just think about it? He really is different this time."

For the next several months gifts arrived for Graham from a halfway house in Arizona. A dozen balloons. A necklace made of Indian beads. A powder-blue satin baseball jacket with a pink flamingo embroidered on the back. It was the ugliest thing I'd ever seen. Graham lived in it. "This is from your uncle Michael," I found myself saying. Somewhere, in a quiet place in my gut, it seemed that something *was* different. It felt like it was time.

I wrote my brother a letter. It was hard to know what to say. It had been decades since we had any good ol' jumping-on-the-bed days to refer to, and even those had been few and far between. Most of our childhood, it seemed, he wanted to kill me.

When I was seven and he was ten, something about the sight of me rankled him so much that carpooling had become untenable. It was decided by my mom and dad, in a scheduled talk that took place in the den (not casually, while teeth were brushed and foam spit into side-by-side sinks), that Michael was at a more vulnerable age for the fallout from their divorce, and that I would be better able to cope with a move. I was relocated to a parochial school in Santa Monica, where we were led in daily classroom prayer, tested for standardized intelligence, and ushered from the school building to the big church each Wednesday morning for chapel. My parents were called in for a meeting. They were told I had an IQ of 164 and had started fainting with some regularity while crossing the schoolyard. I remember my mom looking at me strangely for a while after that, as if trying to read my thoughts. I didn't know what to tell her. I just knew that things occurred to me so much and so fast sometimes, they made my head spin. The following year it was decided I could return to the secular school I had attended my entire life and it was hoped that Michael would learn to control himself.

In my third letter, I extended an offer to my brother to meet my son. Michael flew in the next week. He stepped out of the car, uncertain where to stand or put his hands. Graham, who was normally quite reserved with strangers, ran up and threw his arms around him. Michael returned the hug with gawky joy, unused to either physical contact or children. My mom leaned against the car, closed her eyes and smiled.

"C'mon, Uncle Mike, c'mon," Graham said, pulling him inside. Michael looked back at me, unsure if his invitation included entering my family's inner sanctuary.

"Go on. He wants to show you something."

Maybe, I thought as I watched Michael and Graham walk hand in hand past our threshold, maybe we *could* be some sort of friends. We had never been close, but we *had* overlapped a lot. . . . *"Remember those TV dinners with the pudding cup in the center?" "Yeah, yeah, and how Mom was always late driving carpool and we had to sneak in during the Pledge of Allegiance." "Oh yeah, yeah, and . . ."* I could picture him at my kitchen table, Graham enrapt—*"What happened next, Uncle Mike?"*—and me rolling my eyes affectionately. I heard laughter from inside the house and thought maybe, after all these years, it might be nice to have a big brother.

"Your brother has melanoma," my mom sputtered through the phone two weeks later. "It's malignant. It's already spread to his lungs and they don't know where else."

I suppose the details are never really important, but the

search for them gives us something to say. "How did they find out?"

There was a pause before the answer came. "His roommate fell off the wagon—went on a bender for three days. Michael tried to stay away from him—he tried so hard, but he had nowhere else to go and—he's so ashamed—his landlord found him unconscious. He wanted to go straight back into rehab. I guess they give them a physical when they get there."

"Where is he now?"

"He's coming back to L.A. for more tests. There're some experimental things going on over at UCLA he might qualify for."

"How long will he be there?"

"I don't know. Listen—come to church with me, please. I need you there with me. Please."

I went, once. The church she had immersed herself in since her cancer was housed in a sanctuary that looked to me like an airplane hangar. The reverend bore such a close resemblance to the TV character George Jefferson that I couldn't help but think that at any moment he would pop up and say, "Good Lord, Weezie, I can feel the spirit here with us today!" But the choir, of which my mom was a member, was extraordinary. Their music crept in through the cracks of your toes, and the congregation—a seemingly diverse group made uniform by a love of angel pins and the color purple—clapped and swayed. Shouts of "Oh yeah" and "Sing it, girl" rose up through the packed crowds. It was lively and vibrant, but it was not for me. I was not one to clap and sway. If I were looking for a church, it would have nice wooden pews, straight and neat and warmed in the familiar rainbow of stained glass. But I was not looking for a church.

Lon and Graham were my religion. And writing was my act of faith.

"Pray for him, Heather," Mom said each time we spoke, which was always more often than I needed or wanted. "I need to know you're praying for him."

"All right," I said. "Okay," I promised, knowing even as I said it that it was a lie. I didn't pray, and even if I did, Michael wasn't going to make it. It wasn't personal, it was medical. He had stage-four melanoma, the deadliest form of skin cancer there is. It had a 99 percent fatality rate. The facts were the facts. Facts were the truth. And I believed deeply in truth.

The year dragged on, and so did my brother's cancer. My mom hated the doctors for not giving him any hope and cursed the system that refused to pay for his medical expenses while covering every illegal alien in the state. It was the first undemocratic thing I'd ever heard her say. Michael's body slowly withered as a bloody purple boil the size of a softball grew on his neck. They said it was too dangerous to lance; he had to wrap it in Ace bandages just to keep it from rubbing against his clavicle. Lesions grew all over his body; wearing clothes became unbearable. For the last several months of his life, he shuffled his naked death-camp bones around the subterranean bedroom of our mother's condo, chain-smoking and letting the ashes fall where they would, transfixed by the television from dawn to the broadcast sign-off tone.

I would spell my mom when I could. She was floundering

26

and spent, and I wanted some time for closure. But Michael wanted *Hawaii Five-0* and *The Andy Griffith Show*. He'd let me sit with him and change the channel, but he didn't want to talk about the meaning of life or where he thought he was going in the next phase or what he wanted us to take from his short existence on this planet or of god. He wanted his pillow repositioned and his *TV Guide* fetched and someone to run up to the liquor store and get him a Häagen-Dazs bar. "I said the vanilla kind with almonds—could you just go back, please, and get it right?"

That September, Lon and I had planned a three-week driving trip along the southeast coast before Graham started preschool. I went to see Michael, to say my good-byes. He was a faint presence. As I turned to leave, Michael lurched upright, vocalizing with a strength that was not his own. "Have a good time," he said as if it were a matter of biblical proportions. "Please"—he softened, smiling with bright, clear, luminous eyes—"you and Lon and Graham, be a happy family, okay?"

"Okay."

We were in Florida when the call came three days later. My brother was dead at the age of thirty-three. There was only one explanation I could comprehend: Someone knew he wasn't going to be able to find happiness this time around; someone was kind enough to put him out of his misery.

I would take time out to cry every day, but I made good on my promise. Michael would never know the simple pleasures of splashing in a wading pool with a toddler, or counting cows through a train window from Ocala to Savannah. He would never hold a woman who was his wife amidst the tall sea grass of Okracoke or put his arms around a boy who was his son and show him how to cast a line out into the almighty seas off Cape Hatteras. I loved it there, my days spent perched on a salt-cured deck chair looking out past the turbulent ebbs to infinity. I loved it from the start, from the very first time Lon brought me to this remote strip of North Carolina shore.

"This is my favorite place in the whole wide world," I said one day, hugging Graham in warm terry cloth.

"How come you like it so much?" he asked.

"I don't know." I stopped, but the answer bubbled up and spilled out in spite of me. "I guess it's because this is the closest I ever come to feeling god."

He leaned back further against my chest and replied simply, "Me too."

Someone was always being tested for something: glaucoma or cavities or cancer. By the time Remy was born, I was stationed by the phone almost weekly for word that the innocuous had indeed turned fatal. Lon had a mole removed. Graham had a checkup and they drew blood. Remy received her second DTP vaccination and we watched to see if she would be the one kid in half a million to die from it. I had a Pap smear. Lynne had her first mammogram: "I know a girl who got it at thirty-two. . . ." My mom went in for her quarterly cancer check. I called every other day for the next ten days to see if she'd heard yet. When she did—when she

28

knew for sure she was fine—she forgot to call and tell me, so I worried for a few days longer than she did.

Then there was Lon's vasectomy. It had been the last procedure done through our old medical group. We had then switched health insurers and signed up with a new family practice physician. The first appointment would be Lon's, as he went in to have his dead sperm duly noted.

"They're still swimming," he responded with a hint of pride upon his return from the doctor's.

"Still?" I said, making a split-second decision that sex would have to be put off a while longer, because I was never sticking that diaphragm in again in my life.

"She also said something about my white count."

"What? What did she say about your white count?"

"It was kind of high. There was some blood there or something, too. She said something about the—what's that thing called? It starts with a *p*?"

"Prostate?" I uttered numbly. "She's concerned about your prostate? You have a high white count in your prostate? What does that mean? Did she say what that meant?"

"I don't know. She's running some tests."

Well, of course, I thought. *It's perfect. It'll be Lon. He's next. They'll take my husband and leave me with his two children, the son who'll grow up to look just like him and the daughter he wanted more than anything in the world. "Your father's last living gesture before his prostate gave out was to bring you into the world, little Remy," I'll tell her one day when she's old enough.*

"Hello, this is Nora Vasquez—Dr. Vasquez. I saw Lon last—"

"I know who you are. Is he okay? Were his tests okay? Is everything okay?" I said in one quick outburst.

"Oh, he's fine. He still has quite a few sperm floating around, but everything else was clear. We'll check the sperm again in a few months."

"Okay," I said, but it was not. "Fine," I added, but that couldn't have been further from the truth. The outcome didn't seem to matter anymore; it was the tests, the uncertainty, the waiting to hear. That alone had taken on an insidiously lethal power. I was thirty-three, an age which my brother had proven was well within death's grasp. The collective heap of anxiety had grown unavoidable, creeping into my craggy, unused brain like bacteria in an open wound. My fears would no longer dissolve with a sunny pathology report; instead they left a residue that clung and mutated and swelled. I couldn't pick up the phone without hearing about someone's mom or dad having bone cancer or skin cancer or a stroke. A fourteen-year-old boy who lived down the street got a brain tumor and was dead within a year.

The L.A. sun seemed cruel to me now. I sat in a tattered lawn chair, studying the heavy-duty canvas eroded by the very sun we were sitting under, and calculated the longevity of our sunscreen. *Three bad burns,* that's what they say. Three bad burns in childhood would do it. I swatted at the dread with a string of opalescent bubbles. Remy smiled and tried to pop one with her hand. Graham chased a big one down the street, whacking at it with an old curtain rod. "Not too far, honey. I want you where I can see you." His blond hair flashed in the hot sun as he ran farther down the block.

"C'mon back. I mean it." He turned his head, eyes like sparklers, and kept running. "Now, honey. Now, Graham. Get back here!" I built to a shout, grabbing Remy and heading down to the corner after him, one eye scanning the sky for helicopters, one ear poised for the telltale shriek of fleeing tires or passing gunfire. *"Now!"*

The danger that summer was not confined to my head.

A decade-long gang truce in the nearby Oakwood section of Venice had turned suddenly deadly. They were no longer keeping things in their own little mile-square patch. They were out, cruising, staring people down, shooting each other on the streets we traveled en route to the video store. The "black on brown" turf war became front-page news. The death toll had reached seventeen. We took the kids to Florida to visit Lon's parents. I weighed heavily the decision to check Remy's car seat through with the baggage, knowing that a baby held in a lap would be the first to catapult through the sold-out flight. At night I tossed and flailed in the thick summer heat and envisioned an age-old mole on my leg making subtle and undetectable changes. I rose to check it again and again, certain that the cancer was spreading as sleep eluded me. *Call now*—calm down—*call the doctor, wake her up*—sleep, just sleep—*make an appointment, go straight from the airport*—it's fine, it can wait. I knew it didn't really matter when I made the appointment. It was already too late. It was out of my hands. We were all strapped into a loose-screwed 747 and one way or another we were going down. It was as near as the next blood test, as real as the next vision. It didn't matter if you tried hard, if you did the right thing, if you led a dignified life, if your motives were pure. It was irrelevant if you loved deeply and well, if you devoted yourself to your family, if you ate all your vegetables or taught your children to eat theirs. Cause and effect was a principle that was failing to re-prove itself in modern times. I had tried. But it made no difference. There was no more lightness in the world, no grace, no logic, no hope, no master plan. No one was watching over us, goodness was not rewarded, and darkness was all around.

4.

timing

Remy needed to be baptized. There was a page for it in her baby book. Shortly after she was born, I called the only church I knew, the Episcopal church where everyone in my family had been married, confirmed or eulogized over the past fifty years. The church where Graham had been baptized, which was the last time we had been there.

"I need to set up a baptism," I said, as if it were a manicure or a dog-grooming. "What dates do you have this year?"

"Are you a member of the church?" the director of pastoral care asked. Evidently he was new.

"Oh yeah, our family's been going there for years."

"Yes, but do you attend services with us?"

"Uh, no. Not really. We live kind of far away," I protested.

"Well, do you attend a church in your own neighborhood?"

"Well, uh, yeah," I said, thinking of it as more of a stretch than a lie.

"Good," he continued gently. "Because the point of a baptism is to welcome a child not only into God's life, but into a congregation as well."

"But—"

"I think it'll be a lot more meaningful for you and the congregation if you have your baby baptized at your local church."

We had never actually been inside our "local church." It was merely attached to the First Lutheran School of Venice, which was the school where we had decided to send Graham—not for its religious influence (no, least of all that), but because the public school in our area was hugely overcrowded and largely non-English-speaking, and our other option, scrounging up enough money to send him to one of the many trendy, prestigious Westside private schools, the kind I had grown up attending, was, to me, even less desirable. I didn't want Graham hanging out with kids who were left home with a blank check while their parents traveled the globe; I had spent many a late night in those homes.

Lon and I had taken Graham to several fairs at the little Lutheran school and we had always been struck by something about the kids there—something in the way they interacted, something kind. And so we signed on, thrilled to have our son going to school just down the street in a kindergarten of sixteen children, where everyone had a place to grow and thrive and find their niche. "And hey, if he has to do a few coloring projects about David and Goliath, well, what could it hurt?" We had done it and managed to escape with no lasting damage. But tangled up in that thought somewhere was the assumption that maybe, somehow, eventually, sort of, we would start going to church there once in a while, too.

It was bedtime, just before Easter, just after my thwarted phone conversation with the man from the church who would not let me fake it — not this time — when I found myself making preparations. I reached for *The Picture Bible* on Graham's shelf. It had been a baptismal gift and was as yet uncracked.

"You know, honey, maybe it's time to learn a little bit about Easter."

"I know all about Easter. The bunny brings a basket and hides it. Remember last year it was in the shower?"

"Yes, but it has other meanings. There are other parts of it," I said as I fumbled with the book, thumbing blindly. *Where exactly is the part about Easter? Why don't they have this thing indexed by holiday?*

"So what's the other part?" Graham asked matter-of-factly.

"Well," I said, looking up from the book and winging it, "you know about god and the angels?"

35

"They're up in heaven, with Uncle Michael."

"Yeah, that's right. Well, the other thing is that what a lot of people believe is that god had a son named Jesus. And that, um, the story of Easter is that Jesus—" *Jesus what? What's the story of Easter? Oh, yeah, died on the cross, buried, ascended—shit, I can't tell him that.* "Let's just say that Jesus was a really smart guy with a lot of ideas about god and how people were supposed to love each other and stuff, and some people didn't like what he had to say, so they, well, they didn't want him around anymore."

"Why didn't they like his ideas?"

"I don't know."

"What did they do to him?"

"Well, they killed him."

"He's dead?"

"No, actually, I mean . . . well, the big part of the story is that after he died, he came back—"

"He wasn't really dead?"

I had just recently gotten him to understand that when people die they are dead; they don't come back, not ever. "Well, it's kind of complicated, but anyhow, people were really glad to see him again, and, I think we'll save the rest for when you're a little bit older."

I suppose I always knew this day would come. When Lon and I had been planning our wedding, the minister had reviewed the vows we wrote and said, "Hey, guys, would you mind throwing God's name in here somewhere, please?" On the night of our rehearsal, we held hands and made promises and sealed them in the name of a god we wouldn't know from Adam, but nonetheless I felt it, like a warm ocean breeze. I looked up at the cross and was overwhelmed with a sense of something huge and eternal and sacred, of entering—*what? What is it?* A bouquet of gift ribbons was shoved in my hands by a well-meaning bridesmaid and the moment was gone. Five years later, as Lon and I and Rob, the godfather, stood up for Graham at the baptismal font, that intense, unfamiliar feeling had reappeared. The reverend this time was a strong, no-nonsense woman who gave one of the most inspiring sermons I had ever heard.

"She was awesome," Lon said in the car on the way home.

"Yeah, really. Amazing." And then we were silent for a bit. "You think we would ever want to like, you know, come back here—you know, once in a while—just to hear her?"

"I don't know. Maybe. It's kind of hard to get past the whole Jesus thing." Even though we had never in our seven years together talked about religion, I knew exactly what he meant.

"It's kind of a big part of it, isn't it? I mean, you can't just work around it, right?"

"I don't think so. They did name the religion after him and everything," Lon said.

I had wondered from time to time about the religious education of Graham and any other children we would have. I'd fantasized about gathering up a bunch of neighborhood kids for an all-day playdate/seminar. All the parents would chip in to cover the costs and we'd invite a Buddhist, a Muslim, a Jew, a Protestant—one of everything—to come by and explain why they believed what they did, give the kids a nice broad sampling, but I knew even as I thought it that it was not a realistic exposure to anything. Now I had a son starting parochial school in the fall and a daughter who needed a place to be baptized. The words "Yes, you do have to wear a tie" flew off my tongue like a commandment, and off we went to church for the first time ever as a family.

It was time.

The church was simple and cheery, with warm wooden pews and handmade felt banners. We sat three rows from the back. Lon's was the only tie there. The pastor saw us and came bounding down the aisle. "Hi, I'm Ken. Pastor Ken. No, no—call me Ken. Glad to meet you," he said with a firm shake and a smile, learning all our names on the spot.

Standing there in the cozy church, looking up through stained glass, across at Lon holding Remy and singing something about lambs, and down at Graham in his cleanest shirt, I started to cry, which I thought was odd because no one was getting married. Pastor Ken picked up a Super Soaker and called all the kids up for a talk about water's bountiful uses—fun and baptism being two of them. Why we were really there I couldn't say, but when we left I stated quite firmly, "We'll go once a month for a year. Once a month is not going to kill anyone. After that we'll evaluate."

Graham never asked about the things that were discussed in church that summer. But two days after kindergarten began he turned to me in a midair jump on the bed and exulted,

"Hey, Mom, did you know that wherever I go, Jesus goes with me?"

My response was a dead-still monotone. "Really."

Meanwhile, I scavenged for clues, scanning resource books—but not the Bible itself—partly curious, partly suspect, partly afraid that Graham would come home with a question that I couldn't answer. Was it possible these Lutherans were going to turn around and shock me? Was it possible that all my gut instincts about the goodness of the school and the church were wrong—that as we spoke my son was being told to sit down and shut up or god would whack him upside the head? Everything I had seen or sensed told me no, but what if I was wrong? *What if they were right?* The introduction to the biblical section of *The Dictionary of Cultural Literacy* stated, "No one in the English-speaking world can be considered literate without a basic knowledge of the Bible." I added that to my lists of rationales for exploring more deeply.

I was, bit by bit, Sunday by every fourth Sunday, unclenching my fist, extending my fingers in a willingness to believe, but there was nothing to hold on to. I liked our little church and our pastor, I found no one in the entire congregation with two heads, and yet I could not make the leap. The world was filled with pleasant, superficial experiences; I didn't need church to be one of them. I grew frustrated and scared, uncertain where I would turn if I journeyed down this road at long last and found at the end of it nothing still. *Tell me how.* There was only one way it could happen. *Help me.* Only one thing I could imagine that could jolt me out of the land of self-sufficiency into the great unknown, into believing, feeling, embracing as you would your child or your spouse some entity known as God and Jesus who was real, who existed today, now, in this world, in this age of righteous agnosticism and slippery metaphysics. *Only one thing.*

It was Sunday morning. Graham was going to sing with his class in the Cherub Choir at the eleven o'clock service and we were all excited. Lon woke up before we heard anything from the baby monitor and went into the bathroom. Graham raced in and shook me. "I think Remy's having a poop or something," he said. It was not unusual to hear a report from him about his sister; since the day Remy was born, the very first thing Graham did upon waking was to rush to her side.

"Tell your dad. He's already up," I groaned, and rolled back over.

A few minutes later Lon returned with Remy in his arms. She was bundled up in a comforter. Her body was twitching in synchronized spasms. She was pale and totally nonresponsive. Her eyes were ratcheted to the far right, dead as iced cod.

"This is not good," Lon said. "I thought maybe she was cold at first, I took her in the bathroom, I put her near the heater, but then I—"

"Go call Vasquez," I said, taking Remy in my arms. Except for the twitching, her body felt like a mannequin. "Graham, get dressed, now," I shouted, slipping on my pants with one hand. I looked closely at Remy's eyes. It was not good. "Hang up the phone. We're going to Emergency. Let's go," I called out as I plowed through the house, grabbing diaper bag, shoes, my son. "I'll hold her, you drive."

"She should go in the car seat," Lon said.

"I can't deal with all those straps."

"Here," he said, peeling her off me, "you drive." Our neighbor came out front to wave. I did not wave back. I realized as I rounded the corner that he would know something was terribly wrong—that within hours the whole street would be waiting and wondering.

"You just went through a red light, Mom," Graham said from the seat beside me.

"It's okay, it's an emergency," I said, turning back to check on Remy at each forced stop. "Remy! Remy! Look at me, look at Mommy, can you look at Mommy?"

I pulled into the parking lot at Santa Monica Hospital and jumped out to announce her arrival. The emergency team moved quickly. She had a fever of 102.7°, not exceptionally high, but they said that a rapid spike could trigger a seizure like this. She smelled terribly of feces. I was certain she was sitting in a huge diaper of diarrhea, but when we stripped her down there was nothing. Her body stopped twitching; her eyes seemed free to move about, but didn't. She lay deathly still on the table as they checked her. Lon took Graham out to the waiting room.

"Remy! Remy!" I urged loudly. "Mama is right here, baby, I'm right here. Everything's going to be all right, okay? It's okay, baby."

"How long did the seizure last?" the ER doctor asked.

I couldn't really say for sure. I didn't know how long she had been having it before we found her. We knew it had to have been at least ten minutes. It might have been twenty. It might have been more. They said the average seizure is three to five minutes. They moved more quickly.

"We need to do a spinal tap to check for meningitis," the doctor said.

"Meningitis? How in the world would she get meningitis?" I asked, my mind reeling. *We're a nice clean family. We're great parents. She's not in day care. How in the world would our daughter get something as creepy as meningitis—whatever that is?* He started to tell me about the risks of the spinal tap, but I interrupted. "She has to have it, right?"

"Meningitis is very serious and very fast-moving. We need to do this as soon as possible."

"Well, do it, then. Just do it."

They asked me to leave the room. They said it was best. She didn't seem to be that aware of my presence anyway. I found Lon in the waiting room. We were both too scared to look at each other for more than an instant. I tried not to cry in front of Graham but it was impossible. "Mama's scared, baby. Mama's really scared." Lon took Graham to get something to eat. I called Lynne from the pay phone. She had watched Remy for a few hours the day before. "Did she eat anything weird? Did she fall? Did anything unusual happen at all?" Lynne said no to all the above and raced right over.

Then I called the church. "Please tell them that Graham

42

won't be there to sing today, and——" The tears were starting to come hard. "Please ask Pastor Ken to pray, ask everyone to pray for Remy——R-E-M-Y——Davis. Please, she's in the hospital. I think she might be very sick."

Lynne took Graham back to her house. Lon and I went back into the exam room. The spinal tap was complete, but the doctors looked concerned; they'd stuck a three-inch needle through her skin into her spine and she hadn't let out a peep. Now they wanted to do a chest X ray. "This kind of thing happens, right? I mean, you see it, right?" I said, hounding the ER nurses. "Babies have these seizures and then they come out of them, right? They come out of them okay, don't they?"

It had been over twelve hours since our last feeding and my breast milk was leaking everywhere. Someone brought me a pump and showed me how to use it. Lon stayed in the exam room with Remy——it was better that way. His mind didn't work hypothetically. As long as the seizure had stopped and she was in no obvious pain, he was content just to hold her.

The ER doctor tracked me down in the little room where I sat bound to the strange milking contraption. The chest X ray was clear, but her blood test showed an elevated white count——a sign of infection. They had started her on a high dose of IV antibiotics.

"So she's going to be okay, right? I mean, she's got a little infection that we can treat, right? I mean, you work in the ER——you see really sick people every day, and she's not like——"

"Don't misunderstand me," he said flatly. "Your daughter is not well. Your daughter is quite ill."

I returned to my pumping. *Have to keep my milk up, she'll want to feed when she's feeling better.*

When I went back into the ER she was sitting on Lon's lap cradled in his arms, looking up at him—sort of. "She held my finger," he said.

"Really?"

"She turned her head toward me a little."

"Rem . . . Remy. Mama's here. Can you look at Mommy?" She continued to look forward and up, in the vicinity of Lon's chin.

"And during the X ray, she made a noise," he added proudly. "Didn't you, Rem?" In my short absence they had forged a bond that I was not a part of.

"Good," I said, but I was no longer listening, concentrating instead on the doctor as he rattled off numbers and statistics into the phone. He hung up and rejoined us. "Her spinal tap was clear—there is no apparent evidence of meningitis or encephalitis."

"Oh thank god," I cried, then boasted, "and she squeezed Lon's finger. She looked up at him."

"Good. That's good. These are all good signs. I am still waiting to talk to the doctor on call in your medical group. He'll need to review her case," he said, then disappeared.

The clouds seemed to be parting. We had been there three hours and she'd gone from nearly comatose to slightly responsive. *She just needed some antibiotics, that's all. We'll take her home, give her some antibiotics, she'll get some rest. This is not going to be a tragedy. The end is in sight. We're not going to be one of those families you read about in* Redbook.

The doctor returned. "We've decided we'd like to check her in for a few days for observation." The seizure had stopped, but they wanted to know the cause. We would later discover that this was an especially vigilant step; the more likely procedure in a case like Remy's would have been to diagnose febrile (fever-based) infant seizure and send her home with instructions to watch and wait.

An orderly wheeled us up to the pediatric floor. It was the blink of an eye, the seven and a half months that had passed since we had last been wheeled through hospital corridors. Then, there had been balloons and flowers. Then, people had smiled and waved and leaned in for a peek. Now, they looked busy, passing quickly, not looking at Remy, not looking at me. I held her tight as we rounded a corner. She was not much stronger now than she had been at one day old.

The halls were bright and fresh and mostly empty. It was a new hospital, a teaching hospital. We were deposited in a huge room at the end of the floor with a window seat, a rocking chair, a spacious sink area and a private bathroom with shower. I noticed a collection of take-out menus pinned to a bulletin board on the wall and realized that someone had stayed here long enough to settle in, grow bored of the food, and think to order something else.

A freckly, raspy-voiced nurse with a large lip sore blustered in to greet us. "Hewo thewa, baby Wemy. Aren't you such a cutie-wootie-pie?" Remy had never been spoken to like that in her life, but she was not in any condition to argue. She lay very still in her stainless-steel industrial crib as the nurse prepared her IV. "We're going to start her on some fluids. She's very dehydrated. Better put these guard rails up—kids this age, it's all fluids. Get some fluids in 'em, they start leaping right out of the crib. You just wait. Can I get you some juice?"

Lon and I nodded and she was gone. Remy lay on her back like a capsized sail—flat, heavy, all future movement hinging on which way the winds might blow. She turned her head, amoeba-like, to look at Lon. He was her focal point. I hovered on the other side. After a while, she turned and looked at me, too. Her left leg was pulled tightly in toward her belly. I smoothed it out, holding it flat for a bit as if to set it. Moments later, it tugged reflexively back toward her chest.

"What do you think?" I asked Lon.

"It's definitely clenching up."

"Yeah, but you know, this is the leg she used to bend a lot early on. You remember when we used to change her diaper, this leg always pulled in more? You know how when they don't feel good, they revert a little bit. Probably it was bent like this in the womb. I think that's what it is. A reflex." And then I grew silent. "It was this leg, wasn't it?"

We hung over the crib and stared at her. Lon held her hand and I continued to iron out her left leg and we both fought back fleeting bits of random medical facts—*isn't that what happens to stroke victims? Don't they freeze in weird positions?*—and wondered if our perfect, beautiful girl would be forever like a character in an Edvard Munch painting.

The on-call doctor from our medical group arrived about one in the afternoon to examine her. We pointed out the left leg, but it was not the left leg he was concerned about. "Has the right side been this flaccid the whole time?" Lon looked at me as if I would know, but I did not. "She doesn't seem to be using her right leg or arm much. See?" He tapped at her right knee. It didn't flinch. "Has it been this way all morning?"

We couldn't really say. We had been so preoccupied with the left leg, we hadn't much noticed. He continued to check her physical movements. It was quite obvious: Her right leg was about 50 percent of her left in skill, coordination and strength. Her right arm had not even moved.

"Isn't that, you know, normal after a seizure like that, that her body would be a little tired?"

"It's not abnormal. We often see side effects for up to forty-eight hours," he said. Lon and I exchanged relieved glances. "Still, I'd like to call in a neurologist. I'd like to get one over here as soon as possible."

Neurologist... *why?* ... neurologist... *what for?* ... neurologist ... *oh my god, they think there's something wrong with her brain.* "But you think it's just a febrile seizure, right? That this is just a little slowing left over from a febrile seizure? You said that some slowing wasn't abnormal, right?"

"I'd say it's about eighty-five percent certain that this is just a febrile seizure, and that the likelihood is she'll regain this movement. But I'd like to get the neurologist's opinion. So let me go call her, all right?" and he was gone.

No, I thought, *it is not all right.* I flung myself over the

47

crib. I kissed her chest, rubbed my nose along her collarbone, tickled her right underarm with my lips. *Move, goddamn it!* I ran my tongue along the side of her rib cage. A small palm nudged my ear. *Ha!* She pawed my hair with both hands, opening her mouth as if to chew it, not enthusiastically, not with playful delight, not with anything more than a newborn reflex, but nonetheless, the tasks were executed. I flew down the hall to the doctor. "She grabbed me with both sides, she grabbed me. She can use her right arm just fine. She just doesn't want to right now. She's tired. But she can. Tell the neurologist she can."

Don't anyone put "brain-damaged" on my daughter's chart.

The neurologist was not as impressed as I was. She ordered a CT scan to get a closer look. They gave Remy Valium so she wouldn't wiggle too much during the test; they didn't want to knock her out completely because it would make it harder to gauge her progress. We escorted the crib down to the basement. The radiologist was annoyed to see that his Sunday rush patient was a baby — "They're so difficult to keep still" — and even less pleased to see her parents hovering.

The CT machine is a metal silo with a tight core into which bodies are fed. The radiologist batted me away as I laid Remy down on the plank. He strapped her down in three places, her eyes wide open and taking in — what, we didn't know. I felt as if my heart had been ripped out of my chest and thrown across the room while I sat handcuffed to a chair. "Mom and I'll be right out here, Rem," Lon said as we were herded into the other room. The radiologist pushed a button.

A conveyor belt rolled her into the cold metal drum like a drawer closed shut at the morgue.

Lon and I stood with our backs to the video readout as the neurologist interviewed us and took probing, sidelong glances. "Was Remy born prematurely?" she asked, glancing casually past my left ear at the screen. "And you say her head was fixated to the *right* side?" she continued, writing down the answers on a tiny white scratch pad without ever looking down at the page. "Did you notice a bluish tint to her lips or skin at any time during the seizure?" I struggled to read her face, to catch the reflection of my daughter's brain in her bifocals. I could have turned to look at the screen, but I didn't know what I was looking for, and I certainly didn't want to find it.

The neurologist walked us out to the hallway. "Well, I'm not seeing anything alarming. I'd like to get an EEG done on her, but I'm pleased with what I've seen here so far. Let's get her back upstairs. We can talk more after the EEG."

Remy was still weak and mildly sedated when the EEG guy came up. I could hardly imagine a healthy, active baby sitting still long enough for a test like this. First, conductive gel is smeared at key points around the skull—in Remy's case, in sixteen different places. Then wires are mashed into the gel and connected to a monitor that scans and interprets the electronic activity in the brain. The preparation alone took nearly half an hour. Remy never lifted a finger to swat away the goop or the coated metal strands that framed her face like a Raggedy Ann wig.

"Good thing she's being so still," he said. "These little guys can be tricky."

The neurologist arrived to pore over the sheaf of scrawly zigzags. "You see this flat part here?" Doctors, I would learn, are forever offering to have you take a look at things they spent ten years learning to read themselves. Lon and I scooted around the ream of paper and squinted. "This flat part here indicates a portion of her left temporal lobe. This left side controls movement on the right side, explaining the slowing we're seeing there. In all likelihood, this is where the seizure originated," she said.

"But that's normal after a febrile seizure, right? Some slowing, right?"

"It's not abnormal," she responded.

This is another thing I would learn about doctors: They use the English language with a complete disregard for nuance. If I were asked that same question by a nervous parent, I might say, "Oh yes, we see it all the time," or "Of course, there's almost always some physical fatigue in the first forty-eight hours," or a short, sweet, encouraging "Absolutely." But doctors, lovers of science and aliens to poetry that they are, will, ninety-nine times out of a hundred, say, "It's not abnormal."

Remy finally nodded off around four o'clock. Lon and I took stock. "Well, so far, so good. No meningitis. The CT scan looks good. She hasn't had a fever for over six hours without Tylenol. It's just a febrile seizure—people have them all the time. I've heard of babies who have one and never have another." Throughout the day we had talked to so many friends who knew kids who had had them, it was starting to seem downright ordinary.

When Remy awakened, I could sense her range of motion making subtle improvements. I lifted my shirt and she fed capably. She was slowly regaining strength. Her personality was not emerging, but I could sit her in my lap and she could hold herself upright with little support. I broke off a piece of a saltine and held it out to her. She took it from my hand, gummed it, passed it to her other hand, then tried to feed it back to me. I raced down the hallway to the nurses' station, shouting, "She held a cracker!" to a group of previously occupied medical professionals. "Then she passed it from one hand to the other on the first try. That's a very fine motor skill. She's only seven months. Babies don't even usually do that at all at seven months. Make sure that goes down on her chart, okay? Make sure the neurologist knows."

The neurologist reappeared a few minutes later. "Did you hear about the cracker?" I said, leaping up to include her in our celebration.

"No. What?"

"She fed herself a cracker—passed it back and forth. I mean, she's still not really herself yet, but her fine motor skills are perfect—you know, if you were worried about her brain."

"Good, that's great. Listen, I've just been conferring with the radiologist. He thinks he sees something on the CT scan. I think it's just a strange angle where her bone is jutting out. But he thinks we should do an MRI. That's the only way to get a definitive picture. I'm ordering one for first thing

51

tomorrow morning. I'm also going to start her on an IV of acyclovir on the off chance that what he thinks he sees on the scan could be a lesion of herpes encephalitis."

"I thought we ruled all that out this morning," Lon said, trying to focus.

"The spinal can only give a preliminary negative. It's not absolute. I don't think that's what we're dealing with here, but encephalitis is very deadly and very fast-moving. It's best for us to cover her with the acyclovir until we can rule it out for sure."

It was then I knew that we would not be turning back. The tunnel would have to be entered. The day before, I lived in the normal world. I had normal, healthy kids and the luxury of complaining about unavailable sitters and the occasional ear infection. But twelve hours had changed all that. I was not going to be one of those people anymore. I was going to learn the language of fatal diseases, blood counts, lab tests, brain scans. Things I had only heard of on TV. Sections in baby books I had flipped frantically past, as if touching the pages of dark possibilities might bring them on.

"Tell him she's doing much better. Tell him about the cracker, okay?" I said to Lon as night fell and he left to pick Graham up.

That day I became the mother of a child whose outcome was uncertain. I would not be going home to a warm bath and a glass of wine and a heavy "what a day" sigh on the couch. I would be spending the night in a hospital room with a frightened, wounded baby whose right side had gone limp, whose left side still resorted to paroxysmal clenching, whose deep blue eyes looked up at me with familiarity but no spark.

My mom arrived at eight-thirty. I had prepared myself for her to be frightened, even hysterical; it had always been the nature of our relationship that she would collapse and I would hold her, but when she walked into Remy's room that night—on time, even—she was calm, meditative, almost upbeat. "Everything's going to be just fine," she said. "I know that she is in her perfect place and that everything is as it should be." Remy seemed determined to show her "Moo" that she *was* fine; for the first time all day she pushed up on all fours in the crib. *Look at me, I'm okay, I'm great,* her red, wincing face cried out. "Oh, Remy, I'm so proud of you, you're so strong and healthy and well," my mom praised with clasped hands. But the effort was overwhelming. Remy toppled over and dissolved into tears. She could no longer look at her Moo without screaming. I pulled her from the crib. She buried her head in my arms. "It's okay, baby. You don't have to do so much. We'll just take our time."

"Remy . . . ," my mom said in a soothing tone, but that was as far as she got. Remy flung an angry eye at her and wailed.

"It's okay, sweetie. It's just Moo. She's just here to tell you how much she loves you," I said, jiggling her and growing tense. Her cries grew more fierce. "Oh, sweet baby, Mommy's not going anywhere. Mommy's right here."

"You want me to hold her?" Mom asked. "C'mon, let me take her—you need a break."

"No," I said, in a knot. Remy writhed and pulled away from any touch but mine.

"Remy, sweetie . . . ," my mom said, trying anew.

Remy began to flail. The uncontrolled physical movement was more than I could bear. "I can't let her cry like this."

"Why don't you let me—"

"You better go," I said, feeling the loss even as I said it.

"Oh, honey . . ."

"I just need to get her settled down, okay? Maybe this wasn't a good idea. Maybe it's just too much excitement for her."

"I'd really like to be with both of you," she said, but Remy screamed louder still.

"I can't. I just can't. Maybe tomorrow'll be better."

It was nearly eleven o'clock that night before I got her calmed down, and then to sleep. For the first time all day, I was totally alone and unoccupied. It was a bottom-of-the-ocean kind of lonely. I rinsed out my mouth and dimmed the lights. The fold-out chair was opened up near the crib. I pushed them together till they touched, then lay down alongside her, reaching my hand up through the cold steel slats to hold her hand. She held it back, but not very tightly. "Everything's going to be okay, baby. We're going to be just fine," I said, but somehow my words lacked the authority that my mom's had carried—like someone who knew the outcome had leaked it to her. There was a moment where I thought I would cry—*not now, she needs you rested.* I covered my head with a pillow to block out the peripheral fluorescence and prayed only for sleep.

The next seven hours seemed like a year. The night nurse had taped some sort of pulse-reading device to Remy's toe that made it glow red like E.T.'s finger and caused a shrill beeper to sound every time she moved, which was often. She thrashed about — pain, nightmares, disjointed circuitry, no one knew — but nurses appeared with thermometers and IV drugs and Tylenol, shining their penlights in her eyes every hour on the hour as a precaution and growing perplexed at her refusal to settle in. The mild-mannered resident on the night shift came by, running cold steel instruments along the sole of her foot. He double-checked to make sure that the emergency seizure kit was taped to her crib post and that the nurses were clear on the instructions for its use. I struggled to calm her with breast milk and the steady motion of the rocker. When her lids did close, the movement beneath them was as frantic as a seismograph during an earthquake, and shortly thereafter the inconsolable screams would start up again. At four in the morning the nurses wheeled away the large industrial crib and the fold-out chair and replaced them with a single adult bed with side rails. We lay down together and slept entwined for over an hour before it started up again — the jagged cry — and with it, daylight.

5.

knowing

Remy's MRI was scheduled for "sometime that morning."
She was as ragged and fussy as she had been all night. Her
only solace seemed to be at my breast. She would look up
at me as she fed, but she did not grab my hair, she did not
fist my nose, she did not whip her head back to let out a sat-
isfied "aargh," she did not try to stand up and crawl away,
taking my nipple with her; these were the things I had come
to know and love about my robust seven-and-a-half-month-
old daughter. These things she was not doing. I looked down
instead into the sweet, birdlike gaze she had offered me as a
two-month-old. "Where are you, Rem? Are you there? Are
you still in there, baby?" I whispered.

A nurse popped her head in. "They're almost ready for her. I'm going to go get the sedative now."

"Okay, whenever you're ready," Lon answered. His eyes seemed like the only safe place left in the world. I clung to his gaze, unable to speak.

"Tttthhwwwww!"

Without warning or explanation, Remy whipped her head away from my breast, sat upright, gave her dad a frisky smile and razzed him. He razzed her back, bolting to her side. "Hey, Rem." He smiled like a great wave of sunlight. She grabbed his hair, tugging and pulling and trying to stuff his head in her mouth. She turned to me and touched my teeth. "Teeth, baby. Mama's teeth," I told her. She touched her own three white pearls with proud recognition. "Remy's teeth, these are Remy's teeth."

We took her over to the mirror and let her see herself. Her eyes lit up and she cackled like a loon. The nurse opened the door. "Okay, they're—" She saw Remy up and alive. "Aha! There's the little girl I knew was in there. Good morning, Miss Remy." Remy smiled and laid her head shyly on my shoulder. The nurse injected a hypnotic sedative into her IV. Two minutes later she was out cold, not to awaken again for nearly twenty-four hours.

"We saw her. She was here. She was totally here," I said.

"She's back," Lon said, intoxicated with emotion. For an instant we forgot what came next.

The MRI technician was a woman. She asked us to remove any metal we might have on us, especially anything sharp. We entered the scanning room. Our nurse screamed.

57

A forgotten pair of scissors was literally jumping out of her pocket; such is the power of the magnets. The technician asked if the nurse and I could strap Remy in. She was pregnant and needed to take extra caution. At first I thought she meant because of the machine. Then I realized that what she wanted to be careful of was Remy. There must have been some advance call, some "possible unknown deadly contagion" call.

The machine itself looked similar to the CT scanner, a huge cylinder with a tunnel in the center. We strapped Remy in, adjusting her head between two little pillows. She looked quite peaceful. There was a mirror positioned over her face so that when she was swallowed up by the big machine we would be able to see her tiny eyelids from the outside. A button was pushed, and Remy slipped out of our reach. The noise escalated. Remy started to flail almost instantly.

"Pull her out! Pull her out!" I screamed.

Remy was restless from the rude awakening. A dull, rhythmic thump continued as the magnets were in their "holding phase." I decided to ally myself with them, pressing my mouth down on Remy's chest and humming four chords . . . *ah, ah, ah, ah* . . . some angelic four-note pattern . . . *Ah, Ah, Ah, Ah* . . . some universal mantra . . . *AH, AH, AH, AH*. She started to settle. I switched the pattern of my voice to match the machine . . . *badum, badum, badum* . . . raising my voice louder, deeper with each refrain . . . *Badum, Badum, Badum* . . . as if I could meld the audio assault with motherly love . . . *BADUM, BADUM, BADUM* . . . I echoed, until finally I was shouting into her little chest and she was out once more. We sent her back in. The machine kicked into high gear. The timer went on: four minutes and forty-five seconds. That's how long the first image would take. There would be five in all, three without dye and two with dye, injected into her bloodstream to enhance the images of her brain with contrast. 4:30, 4:29, 4:28 . . . She lay as still as glass. The noise was no longer disrupting her. Me, it was driving to the brink. It was like being locked in a room with a dozen jackhammers, each striking the singularly anxiety-provoking note of a colicky newborn. Lon held me tight from behind, swaddling my arms in his as I hopped back and forth from one foot to the other, a manic high priestess, humming, jiggling, frantically hopping. 2:13, 2:12, 2:11. . . . Time passed like a slow, painful death. *If my baby can get through this, then I can goddamn well get through it with her,* I shouted at myself in silence.

"If I wanted to leave, when would I do it?" I finally blurted out.

"There'll be a pause in between each shot," the technician said.

:07, :06, :05. I turned to Lon. "Can you do this? I can't do this."

"Go. It's fine. She'll be fine. I'll stay with her."

"I'll be right out here if she wakes up."

I fled to the small streetside waiting area. I'm not sure it was any more peaceful. In place of the noise, there was the truth: At that very moment a group of experts was standing behind a smoked glass window looking closely at Remy's brain to see if there was something there that shouldn't be. It wasn't just a random check, one of a thousand things you eliminate from your mind each day because what are the odds that your kid would be "one in ten thousand kids who . . ." The experts had just cause for their search. I flung open the glass door to fresh air and found none. The streets were hectic and dusty with construction. *Please, please, please,* I pleaded. Logic would have it that the sentence would continue, *Let the MRI be clean. Let there be nothing there. Let this all be a mistake.* But no—the words that came to me were these: *Please, please, please give me the strength to handle whatever comes.* I found it odd to hear this thought forming in my head. Why wasn't I asking for wellness? Who hopes for problems and the ability to handle them?

Please, please, please give me the strength to handle whatever comes.

I went back inside, scanning for a focal point—a magazine cover, a bug on the philodendron, anything to distract my schizophrenic brain waves. I shut my eyes, then opened them. I stared up at the ceiling, then down on the—There. On the flat charcoal carpet. Laid out at my feet. The word *Center.* Spelled out clear as day. Center? I turned to the window. The words *Magnetic Resonance Imaging* were blocked by some scaffolding across the street. The sun was butting up solely against the word *Center* and speaking to me from the floor. Center. *Please, give me the strength to handle whatever comes.* I heard the shuffling of transitions. Lon appeared in the wheelchair holding Remy. The nurse was picking up some paperwork from the screening room. When she turned around she didn't meet my eyes.

"There's something there, right?"

"Heather, stop it," Lon snapped.

"What? I know. There's something there. Right?"

The nurse could not evade me. "Well, the thing that they thought they saw was there, yes, but you need to talk to your doctor about it. She'll explain everything," she said hastily, then switched gears. "She did such a good job, though, our little Remy. What a brave girl." She was still completely sedated. I held the door open as the nurse wheeled them down the ramp. "Okay, Dad, hold on, we have a bump here."

Remy slept all afternoon while Lon and I waited for the neurologist. It was then I thought about Holland. I had read about it in a letter to Dear Abby a few years back, a hauntingly beautiful fable written by a mother of a child with some sort of birth defect. In it she described the giddy months of pregnancy as a joyous time of planning, like a magical and romantic journey to somewhere you've always dreamed of going. To Italy, yes, Italy. The two of you had always dreamed of going to Italy and you count the days until the birth, which will land you there. But then something happens—something with the train—and you are dropped off in Holland instead. And at first you yell and scream and blame people and insist that someone right this terrible error, but it cannot be righted. Your family will have to stay in Holland after all. You have no choice. And so you start making your adjustments and learning Dutch and figuring out how to walk in clogs. And then one day, you notice the tulips and the windmills and it occurs to you that Holland is not without its charms. It was not what you had dreamed of. It certainly is not as fast-paced or exciting as Italy. It is certainly not the trip you had planned for all your life. But there is beauty there after all. And in the end, you discover that you are glad you came.

I stared at my daughter as she slept, stroking her head, daring to imagine what was buried beneath her skull, and I prepared to go to Holland.

When I was little I loved to fly. I could never understand why people were afraid of it; I had a child's wonderful cocksureness that any plane I was on was a carrier of very precious cargo and, as such, was impervious to disaster. By the time I was twenty-three, I was spending half of each month in the air and on the road, writing, shooting and editing commercials, conducting focus groups and making presentations for a large national retail account. It was the least creative work I had done in my five years in the advertising business, but the responsibility was enormous and the pay sizable; by traditional yardsticks, it was a step up.

There was a meeting one day at our client's corporate headquarters. Five of us flew in from the L.A.-based agency. Several of their top executives were there as well. We needed the CEO to sign off on the first completed commercials of a new campaign. All other phases of the multimillion-dollar effort were on hold, pending his approval, and the CEO, an extraordinarily savvy and engaging man, was not going to be available to us again for several weeks. Just that month he had bested Lee Iacocca to become *Fortune* magazine's CEO of the year, and his calendar was exceptionally full. We were told to come up and they'd work us into their meeting. Twelve minutes later, after wrapping up his own agenda, the CEO headed for the door. I looked to his number-two and number-three and number-four guys, each of whom made in excess of a million dollars a year. Not one of them so much as cleared his throat. I turned to our top brass, men with MBAs and company cars and twenty years of corporate know-how. They busied their soft hands but did not speak. The room was shrouded in an awkward, twitchy silence. It was incomprehensible to me that we had spent three hours and a layover and god knows how much in airfare and we were not going to even attempt to address the business at hand. I waited until he touched the brass door handle.

"Uh, Warren, excuse me," I said, cutting the silence in one fast breath. He turned back; the room grew overly alert. "We brought the new spots with us and we'd really like for you to take a look at them while you're here."

"Oh, good. Make it quick, though." He smiled and sat back down, his chin resting boyishly in his hands, facing the TV monitor. The cassette was yanked away from me by the marketing manager and the two senior account executives, who were now bumping up against the VCR like the Keystone Kops. All told, it took three minutes. Three minutes for him to watch, offer his congratulations and sign off on the entire package, enabling thirty people—including myself—to proceed with their jobs for the next month.

That evening, I was strapped into business class, anxious to get home. There were mild flurries circling the wings and some ill-defined delay being periodically referred to by the captain, leaving me with time to think. *What if* my *time isn't up, but someone else's is?* I sought out the nearest emergency exit. *How could it be that my presence alone is enough to ensure the safety of this plane?* My callow fearlessness no longer held. *I've become one of the herd.* I had breathed in the mythic threat of The Shareholders. *I am now subject to the fate of the masses.* The great joy I had once known—the joy of creativity and imagination and original thought turned into results—was gone.

After that day, it all seemed harder, the ground shakier, and my invincibility less certain.

"Well, it's most likely one of two things," the neurologist said shortly after she entered. She was not one to beat around the bush, which I appreciated. "What we think is that it's a cyst—what we call a hamartoma or possibly a low-grade astrocytoma, probably something she was born with. Most likely benign. I have spoken to the head of pediatric neurosurgery over at UCLA, Dr. Peacock, and he has agreed to see Remy."

"She needs brain surgery?" I countered, stunned.

"Well, that will be up to him and to you. He'll need to see

her first, see the MRI. He may suggest that you just watch and wait for a while."

"Watch and wait for what?" I asked.

"To see if the seizures continue or escalate."

"I really don't need to see the seizures continue or escalate."

"It might be necessary to evaluate her. If that's his recommendation, I suggest you take it."

"What are we supposed to do, camp out in her room? Sleep under her crib? She could have been having seizures all night, for all we know."

"It's highly doubtful that she was having seizures all night."

"Why?"

"It's medically very unlikely that she would be here, doing as relatively well as she is, if she had had multiple and prolonged seizures."

"Great. So you're saying she'd be dead. We never heard a thing, it was only by some total fluke of timing that this seizure occurred when we were waking up, and because of this—this fluke, this bit of luck—she's here. Well, I'm not taking her home to watch and wait only to have her die the second I fall asleep. Let's just get over to UCLA and do it. If there's something there, let's get it out, whatever it is. If that's what we have to do to get back to normal, let's just do it," I said, then remembered that it was not entirely up to me. I looked at Lon, my voice dropping almost to a whisper "Don't you think?"

He said simply, "I agree."

It wasn't until after Lon had spoken that I flashed on all the ways that might have gone. How difficult it would have been if he had jumped in and said, "I demand a second opinion," or "No one's going to lay a hand on my little girl's head," or "I think we should try alternative medicine first." But no, never. We moved through each decision in tandem: me the relentless seeker and assimilator of data, he the calm and steady hand.

"Well, you'll talk to Dr. Peacock about it, see what he says. Some kids have twenty, thirty, a hundred seizures before they even discuss surgery."

"I can't live like that."

"You may not have a choice."

"There's no way."

"If you have to do it, you'll do it. It's just part of being a parent," she said, clipping my skittering wings. There was a silence like a loud pout.

"What's the other thing?" Lon asked.

"Well, we still have not been able to completely eliminate the possibility of herpes encephalitis. It is still possible that the cyst is actually a herpes lesion in the very early stages and that the fever was actually *caused* by the herpes virus itself."

"You mean, as opposed to the fever just being the result of some regular old flu bug or something?" I asked, trying to get clear. It was very important to be clear. I felt as if my understanding of her condition might have a direct effect on the outcome. "As opposed to some bug that caused a regular old fever, which then triggered a seizure because there was a cyst there, which made her more susceptible to having them?"

"Right. So we're going to keep her on the acyclovir until we know more from the lab. We'll also continue to give her the antibiotics—nothing's grown yet in those tests, but we need a full seventy-two hours to definitively eliminate bacteria."

"Yeah, but nothing's grown yet. That's good, right?"

"Yes, and her white count continues to drop, so—"

"So she's getting better? She's not 'sick' sick."

"Probably not. Let's just wait and see. I'd also like to start her on an anticonvulsant, now that we know there *is* something there. I'd recommend phenobarbital, unless you have a problem with that."

"What's wrong with it?"

"Well, some kids it makes hyper, some kids it makes lethargic—some kids do just fine."

"What about the alternatives? What kind of side effects with those?"

"Nausea and vomiting."

"Okay, well, phenobarbital it is," Lon said, and we shared our first laugh in days.

By evening I had learned my new lines and was trying them out on assorted friends and family. "Well, it's a little cysty thing—not big, not big at all. She says it's not right on the surface but it's not too deep, either. And this guy she's sending us to over at UCLA is a real heavy hitter. I mean, this is what he does all day long—operate on kids, just in this area of the brain. This is his specialty. He's The Man, you

67

know. There is this slight chance of this viral thing but they really don't think that's it. They should be able to eliminate that soon." As soon as I hung up the phone, it rang. It was the doctor who had found Remy to be flaccid and requested a neurologist. "So, how're you doing with all this?" he asked genuinely.

"Well," I said, "we're doing okay. Tell me if you think this logic is skewed: She has this little cysty thing she was probably born with. We were lucky enough that at this very early age—before she has many skills to lose or the long-term memory for this to be psychologically scarring—she catches some little bug or something, which triggers a fever, which sets off this little cysty thing, causing a seizure, a pretty long one, long enough to cause some alarm, so you checked her out further. Now we know it's there, so we can have it removed and she'll be freed from much greater problems that would have occurred down the road if this thing was left in there. So really, we are incredibly lucky."

"Boy, you really are an optimist," he deadpanned.

"Why do you say that?" I jumped. "Is there something inaccurate in what I just said?"

"No, it's just that most people who find out that their baby has a brain tumor aren't—"

"Why did you call it a tumor? The neurologist called it a cyst."

"We use those words interchangeably," he explained.

"Well, don't. If they're interchangeable, let's call it a cyst." Semantics plays a very important role in the sanity of an ill child's parents.

*　　*　　*

By Tuesday morning I could see the light. The movement on Remy's right side was at least 80 percent. It was enough not to worry us anymore; enough that, even if it never got any better, it seemed like a minor physical-therapy issue and nothing more. I found her a high chair and watched with delight as she devoured trays full of Cheerios and fat chunks of banana. By late afternoon, the doctors felt confident that the seizure had been triggered by an organic problem — the cyst — as opposed to a viral or bacterial problem. They wanted to do a twenty-four-hour observation test without the acyclovir or antibiotics just to make sure. At midnight all medication would be cut off, except the phenobarbital, which would continue to thwart any seizure that the cyst might cause. If everything went as they expected it to, they would release her Thursday morning, straight to her appointment with Dr. Peacock.

By nightfall Remy was going full steam ahead. I walked her up and down the halls. We studied the Seven Dwarfs wallpaper and labeled their little forest friends: chipmunk, squirrel. Remy pointed to Snow White and I found myself saying, "Beautiful princess." I had a pang about introducing her to that term, then smiled, realizing that my concern meant I was starting to feel secure enough about her future to worry about things like gender stereotypes. I lifted her hand to mine and kissed each finger. It was then I noticed her palm. There was a kind of reddish tear about the size of a corn kernel smack dab in the middle of it. It looked like a scrape. I walked her over to the nurses' station and pointed it out. "Do you think we should put some Neosporin on it or something?"

"Air's the best thing," they said, and wiped it with an alcohol swab to appease me. I took Remy back into the room and tucked her in. I uncurled her little fist to check the scrape. I dabbed it again with alcohol. She caught it on something, I told myself. On a rough edge in the high chair, maybe, or on the side of the crib, I reasoned, although I was hard pressed to think of a single movement she had made all day that would have been big enough to take a chunk of flesh from her hand without my noticing or her crying over it. But the nurses weren't worried, so I decided I shouldn't be, either. I assembled my fold-out sleeper and settled in with the knowledge that the drug-free observation period would begin as we slept and that when we woke up in the morning, we would be almost a third of the way through it. Seven hours closer to clarity.

On Wednesday morning Remy was even more delightful than the day before. I borrowed a rolling infant crib and took her for a speed ride around the floor. She smiled and played to the passersby, not a care in the world. I swung by the nurses' station on the way back to our room. "Do you have any more of those alcohol pads? I want to give this little scrape a wipe-up."

Dr. Vasquez whipped her head around. "What scrape?"

She had come by the hospital to check on Remy's progress. Now she moved in to scrutinize her hand, and scowled.

"Have we done a smear on this yet?" she asked, never taking her eyes off the moist, red unknown.

"No," the three nurses chimed in unison.

"Well, let's do one. That could easily be a primary lesion."

"A herpes lesion on her hand?" I asked.

"It's not the most common location, but they can show up anywhere."

"Wouldn't we have seen it forming? Wouldn't we have noticed it blistering up and everything first?" I asked nervously.

"We looked at it last night," said one nurse. "It was a scrape, that's all. A little scrape," claimed another.

"We've got a baby here with a possible encephalitic brain mass. Let's not ignore the obvious. Do the smear, all right? Stat."

The nurse and I grumbled like scolded children, not quite certain we were right. She pressed a Q-tip into the exposed area of Remy's hand. The swab came up clean, no pus, no ooze, no shed cells—there was nothing to smear. She mashed down harder still. Remy howled in our faces and held us accountable for her pain. The nurse threw up her arms. "There's nothing here. This is not a herpes!" she said in her thick French-Canadian accent, which made the virus sound more like an hors d'oeuvre. "There would be crust and fluid or something. There's nothing. I can't get a smear unless I cut her open and I'm not going to put this little girl through that." They decided that given the lack of "evidence" they could eliminate the possibility of a herpes lesion, and it was all but forgotten.

At two o'clock, the neurologist came in to tell me that after reviewing all of Remy's most recent test results and observing her steady improvement, they had decided to release her that afternoon. "She's far too healthy to be cooped up in a hospital. At this point she'd be better off at home."

"I'm sure she would," I said calmly. "But you said a twenty-four-hour observation. You don't declare a twenty-four-hour observation a success just because the first fourteen hours have gone well. If she's still fine tomorrow morning, we'll go. But I am not taking her out of here before then."

6.

hold on tight

At four-fifteen on Wednesday afternoon Remy started to whine and fuss and bite down hard on my shoulder. *Teething,* I thought, but with no great conviction. "Teething," the nurses said as I loomed outside their station, jiggling her in frustration. My mom was scheduled to bring Graham up for a visit around five o'clock. It would be the first time he had seen either of us in four days. "C'mon, baby, settle down, you need to get some rest now." I couldn't stand the thought of Graham seeing her unhappy. I had no place to put that ache.

We had spoken by phone, Graham and I, but only of mundane things. I didn't know how much he understood, not really, or how it was affecting him. As I sat waiting for him to round the corner, I thought back to something that happened the week before. Remy had already gone to bed. Graham was eating a bowl of ice cream. Out of the blue, he had looked up, shaken his head, and said in a voice nearing awe, "I just can't believe I have a sister."

By the time he arrived, she seemed better. I grinned a lot and asked ordinary questions and tried to read his eyes as we moved into the frigid, germ-free playroom. "So tell me what's going on at school. What letter are you working on now?" He watched her, approaching gingerly, making broad, silly faces, more awkward than I was used to seeing him. "She's kind of tired and everything, sweetie, so, you know, don't expect her to give you her big laugh and everything."

"Want to hear me say the Pledge of Allegiance?" he asked, jumping up on a giant stuffed panda. He recited it without a bobble, and I tried to comprehend the fact that he had grown up four days' worth without me.

"Wow. That's great. So, do you do that every morning now?"

"I don't know. I think so."

"What else? Do you do the Lord's Prayer, too?" It seemed those two things went together.

"How does that one go?"

I hesitated, then began saying it out loud as if it were a mailing address I almost knew by heart. "Our father, who art in heaven, hallowed be thy name. Thy kingdom come, thy will be done on earth as it is in heaven. Give us this day our daily bread, and lead us not into temptation—" *Shit, I think I left a part out.* I continued, concomitantly retracing my steps. "—but deliver us from evil, for thine is the kingdom and the power and the glory, forever and ever. Amen."

"We haven't learned that one yet."

"Forgive us our trespasses," I blurted out. *Why do I always forget that part?*

A nurse came by to commend him. "You did a really important thing, finding your sister like that in the crib—telling your parents right away. You helped save her life."

He grabbed my leg. "Honey, the nurse was trying to tell you something important."

Graham pressed in against me and whispered, "Didn't you say I could have a soda?"

"Sure, absolutely, let's go get a soda."

"And chips."

"Whatever you want." I left Remy with my mom and the nurse and we went in search of the vending machines. "So, listen, do you have any questions about Rem?"

"You think they'll have the nacho cheese ones?"

"Maybe. Is that what you want?"

"Maybe. I'll see what the choices are."

"So, anyhow, I just want you to know that Remy's feeling much better now than when you saw her before—you know, when she had the seizure. They wanted to let her come home today, but we decided, just to be on the safe side, we'd wait till tomorrow." Graham scanned the rows of chips and cookies and candies and mints as I spoke. "So, we'll come home tomorrow, and then in a few weeks she'll probably go

over to a different hospital, where they'll do some things to
fix her up so she won't have any more problems, and then I
think that everything will be okay. I know it's kind of scary
and—"

"You're coming home tomorrow definitely?"

"Uh-huh."

"Remy too?"

"Yep, they just need to double-check a few things in the
morning, that's all. By the time you get home from school,
we'll be there waiting, okay?" I wanted to feel more confident in this promise; I had never lied to my son.

"Okay."

"Are you okay? Is there anything you want to ask me?"

"No."

"Are you worried about your sister?"

"Will you push that one—the Chee-tos, please?"

"I know you must be thinking about it and I just want
to—"

"Mom, Remy's fine. Nothing's going to happen to her,"
he said, as if he knew things that I didn't. "Everything is
going to be all right."

I deferred to his certainty. "How do you know?"

"I just know."

We put Graham and Mom back on the elevator. It had
gone well, I thought. She had held up okay. He seemed to be
coping. I felt better for our time together—happier, relieved.
Remy and I danced down the hall past our dwarfs and our
princess and our forest friends. "One more night, sweet angel, just one more night." She touched her hand to my back

and patted it. "Thank you," I sighed, smiling. I pressed my lips to her cheek. Her skin was like wet August brick.

It was Lon who had taught me that the world would not always move according to my plan. He had taught me patience, forced me to learn it, by having an emotional clock far different from my own.

"I love you," I would say again and again in the early months of our dating.

"Fun evening—enjoyed it," he would reply.

He was not playing games. He knew what it meant to give yourself over and be left for scrap. He knew that those words meant everything, and he would not throw them around like some cheap appeasement. With Lon, I would learn to wait.

The sweet young resident who had been on duty every night since we'd been at the hospital was paged. So was our Dr. Vasquez and the neurologist and the lab. Remy's temperature had spiked to 101.7°. They gave her Tylenol. There was an order to start up the acyclovir again. Stat. People started to shy away when I approached. I called home. No answer.

Doctors and nurses came in and out, looking thrown. I had no smart questions to ask, no bold optimism. It was Lon who made me brave. He didn't have to say a word. He didn't have to do a thing—I could do it. I just needed to have him nearby, there, where he could catch me. Without him, I retreated to much darker corners. I tried again. Still, no answer.

Remy's fever went down quickly and stayed down until eight o'clock that evening, which would be expected with the acetaminophen. Now we'd wait and see how she'd do without it. They ordered another blood test to check her white count and another urine specimen, this time a sterile one.

"What does that mean? What's a sterile one?" I asked, still alone and increasingly terrified.

"We need to insert a needle in through her pelvic region and extract it directly, so that there's no possibility of contamination from the diaper area."

"Haven't we already eliminated a bladder infection?"

"We thought we had, but when a child spikes a fever like this for no known reason, we have to go back to square one. I'm sorry."

"Couldn't it have just been from her teething? From running around with her brother and teething? You know, kids this age run little fevers from these things."

"Yes, I suppose sometimes they do."

But no one was willing to dismiss her fever spike as teething. I asked to go in with her for the urine test. They said no. The only other time they had said no was during the initial spinal tap. Obviously this test would be just as torturous. They carried Remy away to the procedure room and I cracked.

"I can't do it anymore, I just can't—I can't stand all this back-and-forth. I can't be here alone. I just can't," I said to

Lon through tears on the phone when I finally reached him around twenty after eight.

"Listen, can you get someone to come be with you? You want me to call Lynne or Suzie?"

"I want you. I need you to come."

"I'm going to get Graham in bed first. He needs that, I think, to keep things as normal as possible. As soon as he's down, I'll see if I can get someone over here, okay? Where's Rem now?"

"She's in the room with them. They wouldn't let me go in."

There was a long pause. "Well, you know they have to do what they have to do, so just try and stay calm. Get something to eat. Just try and hang in there, okay?"

"I can't."

"Have you eaten? You want me to bring you something?"

"I can't. Please just come now, okay?"

"Heath, we have things we're dealing with here, too, okay? I'll get there as soon as I can."

I thought a thousand things as I waited for Remy to be returned, her shrieks apparent to me from three rooms away. *This is why Lon's vasectomy didn't take.* I could remember vividly the conversation we had right before his surgery.

"There's only one situation I could ever imagine where I'd want to have another one," I'd said.

"If that happens, we'd probably end up divorced. Everyone ends up divorced after that," he'd said.

My mind reeled. *Is that where this is headed? Am I going to lose my daughter and my marriage in one fell swoop? Is it possible that we could actually grow to hate each other? Is that how it happens? Or is the pain just too much to overcome? Would we have joint custody and cordial, leaden discussions at our respective front doors on alternate weekends? Would I become the mother with the dead daughter and the fled husband and the scarred son dumped off early and picked up late—by whom?—by me, the last mother to pull in at the gate, a cigarette hanging out of my mouth, no doubt, racing home to get changed for a date—yes, I suppose that's how it would go—a date, with some alcoholic mucky-muck who'll want me to shave my legs and commiserate about his ex and on the third date—is it still the third date?—go hand in hand for an AIDS test. One febrile seizure and my life is over, is that how it works, goddamn it?*

No. No. Wait a minute, that's not it. It can't be.

What about the sperm? That's why they defied the surgery. Someone knew we would want to have another one.

Someone knew Remy would need to be replaced.

I also thought about my uncle. He had been a neurosurgeon at UCLA but had retired early, throwing his restless brilliance into a series of Ph.D.'s and art forms. He was quite gifted with his hands. When Remy was just two months old, he was alone in a house in Santa Barbara and killed himself. It was Easter Sunday. There was an informal memorial held—not in a church; he despised the Church—but in this final makeshift home, where smack-dab in the center of the courtyard stood a life-size sculpture of a crucified Jesus. "Is that one of my uncle's?" I asked a friend. "Yes, he just finished it this winter." I had asked our neurologist, who had gone to UCLA and appeared to be my uncle's age, if she had known him, and her eyes lit up. "My God, he was one of the most brilliant diagnosticians I ever met." The irony of that kept me company as I waited alone in the dark.

Lon arrived by 9:30 P.M. He rubbed my feet as our now-familiar night resident explained how it had taken three tries, but they had finally managed to puncture her flesh precisely enough, and hold her still long enough, to get their sterile sample. The moment her lips touched my breast she was out.

"I need to get back," Lon said. "I promised your mom I wouldn't be too late. Are you going to be okay?"

"I hate this."

"I don't think she has this encephalitis thing, I really don't. I think you should just go to sleep, let the nurses take care of her for the night. In the morning we'll know more."

"If you've gotta go, just go," I said. He leaned over the crib to offer Remy a—"Don't kiss her," I snapped. "You might wake her up."

Lon kissed instead my taut, turned cheek. "Call me if you need anything," he said, and just like that, he was free. I listened in disbelief as the resident spelled out the revised orders for the night: Remy's temperature would be checked hourly; if at any time it rose to 100°, she would be given Tylenol; if it reached 102°, she was to be given another emergency spinal tap. As I braced myself for that watershed night, I didn't bother to change into a sleepshirt. I didn't fold out the bed or tuck in the sheets. I didn't wash my face or brush my teeth or wind down with the news. I only made one preparation, and that was to pray.

Now, *god,* as a rule, is spelled with a capital *G,* but not by me. Not when it's coupled with "damn it," which, by the time I could drive, was the only way I used it. As an adult—if pressed—I would describe god as something along the lines of "ultimate goodness, loving and light," but it wasn't attached to any "him," nor did it have any sons. I distrusted religion, both organized and otherwise. I owned up to no relationship with any higher power. I did not pray or kneel or turn things over to "him," yet despite all this, I knew. Deep in the heart of wherever these certainties lie, I knew: god was the truth. I knew it, yet I neither sought it out nor embraced it—no, any possibility of that had been destroyed, by the rabid demagogues who called themselves "Christian." As I stood over Remy's crib at midnight, I couldn't say—nor did I much care—what other people believed or how they behaved. I just knew that there was nowhere else to go with pain and doubt this deep. So I clasped my hands and bowed my head and asked god to keep my beautiful daughter safe and cool through the night, to keep me coping and Lon strong and Graham resilient. And I hoped against hope that my tenuous little lower-case *g* would somehow be enough.

There was an especially angelic nurse on duty that night. I had never seen her before. Each hour when she came in to check Remy's temperature she would sit on the edge of my fold-out bed and we would talk, sorting it all out in a way that made it seem positive. When morning broke, I hugged the day nurse and squealed, "She's been afebrile all night!"

This seemed, to me, a huge victory. Remy didn't have to have another spinal tap. Whatever had caused the fever spike the day before was obviously not raging in her system. We would be going home soon after all.

The sun poured in through picture windows. A bird flew by and Remy pointed, tracked it perfectly with her eyes. I guzzled four small cartons of orange juice, shook my head in an ain't-life-grand kind of way and felt certain that my son talked to God.

"Good morning," I heard a familiar voice say, and I turned to find Dr. Vasquez.

"Just coming to see us off?" I chirped.

"Heather, we've decided to transfer Remy over to UCLA. Dr. Peacock can see her over there. We would also like for her to be seen by their Infectious Disease Team." *Infectious Disease Team?* "They're really excellent at . . ." Her words became garbled as I envisioned a faceless mob in matching triple-layer jumpsuits taking notes with thickly gloved hands. ". . . they've already agreed to the transfer." *So, it's a done deal.* "You'll be transported by ambulance as soon as a bed opens up. Probably by lunchtime."

7.

hurry up and wait

By late afternoon there was still no open bed. I'd been to the UCLA Medical Center once—just briefly. For the most part, it lurked in my mind as the turf of dire circumstances, and nothing anyone said that afternoon made me see it any differently. I was told it was very big and hurried and impersonal; that roving hives of med students would swarm the crib at all hours, asking a million questions—the same ones, again and again; that the rooms would be much smaller and darker and more crowded; that the nurses there would be much too busy to sit around and chat with me, as they had here; and that later, when—if—Remy did end

84

up in ICU, I should try not to get too depressed because I'd be seeing a lot of extremely sick kids there. I had to escape.

I rode the elevator down to the lobby. The world seemed shiny and bustling and strange, as if I'd been sealed in a time warp, then set loose in the center of some Huxleyesque office park. There was a gift shop with tiny velvet dresses—navy blue with satin rosettes—displayed in the window. I went in to check the sizes. Three months, six months, three months—nothing bigger. I had forgotten that babies weren't supposed to be in hospitals except to be born. I imagined all the squealing new grandmothers flocking in to buy their red, wrinkled one-day-olds their first party dresses. I was not their target customer. My baby was in twelve-month sizes, and her ever-changing IV accessories wouldn't work with a puff sleeve.

In the corner near the exit was a chapel. It occurred to me to pass by it, but I could not. I approached the kneeling rail, but did not kneel. What would I say when I got down there? For the first time in my life I regretted cheating on my confirmation exam. *Maybe if you'd done your homework, you'd have this kind of information tucked away: "In times of grave danger, appropriate comfort is available in Ichabod, chapter 4, verses 10–15."*

I knew the Lord's Prayer—most of it—but that seemed a little general. I remembered that the world was created in Genesis, which, as logic would suggest, was in the front, and that Corinthians had the ever-popular "Love is not this, love is not that" part. As it happened, I knew it almost by heart, having read it aloud at three different weddings. (At one of them—a big church wedding of a very close and equally emotional friend named Thérèse—I wept so profusely at the dais that Lon now refers to the passage as "Love is not weepy, love is not runny.")

There was a rack of pamphlets on a marble sideboard; I picked out one entitled *When Someone You Love Is Suffering*. I read it slowly. I looked up at the cross. I held my breath. I bowed my head. I pressed my fingertips together and I thought solemn thoughts. But I didn't feel god's presence. I was going through the motions. I was covering my bases. When I left, I was as depressed and terrified as when I came in.

I had wished him dead many times, my mother's lover, Winston. Not because he was black, but because his blackness seemed to cause so much upheaval. One time my wish actually took the form of a prayer. I said it with my hands crossed and my head bowed. I said it out loud. I had come to ask god to get rid of him after finding a package of condoms in my mother's nightstand. I had no idea what they were, but I knew they were something secret and belonged to him and they were here in her nightstand and things were never going to be the same.

My mother met Winston at a UCLA extension course when I was six. I remember him coming to the house and he and my dad having a seemingly civilized chat in my father's study and shortly thereafter my dad telling me he was going to move out because my mom was having some problems and needed to be alone. We moved to a house in a tract on a hill, and I began doing fewer things with the friends I had grown up with. They didn't call anymore, and they weren't free when I called them. It was an entirely different life—an adventure—with my mom single-handed at the helm.

When it came to raising children, her philosophy was simple: "Love them and let them be who they are." The rest of her repertoire was short but sweet: "Do unto others," "Different strokes for different folks," and "Have a great evening"—that's what it always said on the notes she left us at night and stuck to the fridge with a smiley-face magnet. She didn't seem to know, or be able to act on, what would seem like the most obvious truths, like children needing rules or protection or a grown-up in the house at bedtime. But from the day she was born, she knew this: She knew that the money was a lie, and acted accordingly; let the chips fall where they may.

After several years of the interracial scandal my grandparents came to our house for a meeting. It was the first time they had sat in a room with Winston, face-to-face. My grandmother spoke very little but when she did her voice did not sound like the one she used in the receiving line at church. It was the men who spoke most, my grandfather the loudest. There was the distinct sound of a check being torn from its book. I could hear it from behind the door.

My grandparents left, but Winston did not. Shortly thereafter my grandfather died of a massive heart attack that, to this day, my grandmother attributes to my mother's humiliating and inappropriate life choices, choices that were not so simple as black and white. Winston was shy and unspontaneous—he had no knack for children. In the seven years they were together I don't remember having a single laugh in his presence. He gave my mom a diamond ring, but she refused his proposal—gently at first, then, as his desperation grew, in stronger and stronger terms until finally one day, as the holidays came to a close, he got the message, stuck a rifle in his mouth and shot himself.

It was not my fault. It couldn't be. God doesn't kill people on the whim of a young girl (leaving reason to dictate that neither does he save them in answer to her young prayers). It just doesn't work like that. It can't—no, Winston's blood would not be on my small hands. Still, my mom was so sad all alone in the house on the hill, and there were all those dinners to make.

Remy's IV started to leak beyond repair. She had already been through one in her foot and now this one in her arm. It was decided she would need a fresh one before the transfer was made to UCLA, which would be "any time now." It was sunset.

Lon went with her to the procedure room while I picked at cold peas and began dabbling in self-pity. A face appeared at the door. I didn't recognize him at first, but when I did—the instant I did—the tears fell hard and fast.

"What? What is it? Have they figured out what it is? Is it really bad?" Pastor Ken said, rushing to my side.

"She-ee—haass—to-oo—geet—a new—Iii—Veee," I blubbered. "She haa-aates—it. She—ju-uust—haa-tes—it." He cradled me and I sputtered on, "And now we've got to go over there and it's going to be all big and dark and terrible and they're going to be poking her all the time and they probably won't even know her name."

Ken shook his head in disbelief. Unbeknownst to me, he had been a chaplain at UCLA for eleven years before coming to the little First Lutheran Church of Venice. "Well, that's never been my experience. I've never known the doctors and nurses there to be anything but caring and compassionate. I think you're going to be pleasantly surprised when you get there."

"Really?" I peeped. It was the first thing anyone had said all day that made me feel better.

The day after our very first visit to his church, Ken had called us at home. He wanted to stop by for an informal how-do-ya-do at the house one evening, at our convenience, which we determined to be the following Monday. I hung up the phone and ran straight to my neighbor, Lynne. I figured she, being Catholic and the only person I knew who went to church, would know about these things.

"So I mean, what about when you tell them, you know, how you really feel?" I asked, teetering.

"What do you mean?" she said, maneuvering her stroller over a bump.

"I mean about not really being too sure about the whole, you know, Jesus thing. The whole died-on-the-cross-for-your-sins thing—which we're just not into—and the whole idea that if you buy into the Jesus thing, you're basically saying that everyone else, every Muslim, every Jew, every Buddhist, is wrong. I mean, we have a lot of conflicts about all this, and, you know, I'm just not sure how you broach them."

She jerked the stroller to an abrupt stop. "Are you insane?" she said, repositioning the pacifier in her daughter's mouth. "You don't get into any of that. Just tell him you enjoy the sermons and you'll try to get there as often as you can but since you have young kids and everything, you probably can't get there every Sunday. And then you serve him some pie."

"Well, then, I mean, what's the point?"

"There's no point. It's a friendly little thing. A little get-to-know-the-priest."

"Pastor."

"Pastor. It's a social thing, it's not a confession."

"I just feel like we should tell him the truth."

"Trust me. Just serve him the pie, smile a lot and get it over with."

I had planned to bake a pie but I ran out of time. I served Pepperidge Farm cookies and Snapple instead. We were all playing out front when he pulled up in his Subaru wagon. Ken kicked the soccer ball around with Graham and we chatted about art and books and Venice. He threw in a little safe banter about UCLA football, but it fell on deaf ears—the only sports anyone ever watched in our house were surfing and gymnastics. We settled into the living room. He gave us a booklet about Lutheranism and we nodded.

"We've got some real conflicts on the whole Jesus thing," I said as the kids started to get restless and bedtime was near.

"Most people in your generation do," he said.

"We're just not willing to believe that everyone else is wrong. You know, I mean, there are a lot of very wise people in the world, and I refuse to accept that their beliefs are invalid."

"Exclusionism is one of the greatest obstacles facing Christianity today. I struggle with it myself all the time."

"And I mean, there are a lot of people out there doing a lot of really terrible things in the name of religion."

"I know. I agree. You know, there's a book that's been very influential for me in dealing with essentially what you're talking about—people who use religion in hateful ways. It's by Jacques Ellul—you might have heard of him?"

"Uh, no," I said, taken aback. I had thought that preachers had just the one reference book.

"I've got to tell you," Lon chimed in out of nowhere, "if it weren't for the kids, we probably wouldn't be doing this at all." I offered him a wide-eyed glance and a forced smile. *Honey, there's honesty, and then there's turning the knife.*

"C'mon, Mom," Graham said, tugging. "Teeth."

"Well, whatever your reasons, we're glad to have you with us," Ken said, sensing the time and rising. "See ya on Sunday?"

"Maybe," we said in tandem.

"Well, whenever you feel you want to be there."

"Maybe Sunday," I said.

For the first time in my life I thought that maybe—just maybe—a church was not a house of deception. We had spoken the truth and this scholarly man had responded in kind, with warmth, intelligence, and a clear willingness to discuss ideas. He'd left the light on and the door open and said to come home whenever we were ready.

". . . and I've got a good friend who works right there in the hospital—Sister Mary," Ken said, continuing to hold my hand and put my mind at ease as we waited for Remy to come back from the procedure room. "I think you'll really like her—she's a feisty one, has more spunk than anyone I've ever met. I'll make sure she checks in on you. And Jean, from our church—she works right there in the chaplain's office. I talked to her this morning. I told her to be on the lookout for you."

I expected that I would hear screams approaching from down the hall, but there were none. Remy made a sudden and buoyant entrance in her daddy's arms, apparently unfazed by the pale blue IV plug springing out from a vein on the top of her head, a portion of which had been shaved to prevent the tape from tugging at her baby-fine hair.

"Don't ask," Lon said with a smile upon entering.

"What is that thing?" I asked.

"We tried four different veins—this was the only one we could get." He shrugged in a glass-half-full kind of way. "Keeps her hands free," he said, and extended his. "Hey, Ken, how're you doing?"

Ken gave Lon directions to the UCLA Medical Center, then ran out to his car for an old parking pass he had stashed in his glove compartment. "Save ya five bucks." He told us that everyone at church and school was praying for Remy and that, if we wouldn't mind, he'd like to come see us at UCLA just to make sure we got settled in all right. He didn't bring a Bible, not one that I saw, anyway. He didn't say, "Let's join hands." He didn't speak in tongues or palm Remy's newly accessorized head. He gave us some inside scoop and a contraband parking pass and when he left, I felt the abyss from here to the uncharted had somehow been bridged, and that I would not have to cross it alone.

"Did you see that?" Lon beamed at 8:03 P.M. Remy had just crawled a good five feet across the hospital playroom—farther than she ever had before. "That's got to be at least ninety percent on her right side," he said, suddenly keeping track of things like percentages.

"Where are they already?" I growled in response. Whatever calm Ken had brought me was long gone. There was nothing cheery about Santa Monica anymore. The only other people on the floor were a newborn with a mild case of jaundice, a teenager with asthma, and a C-section mom who needed a few extra days to recover. I longed to be around people who were as thick into it as we were—thicker, even. It was unsettling to feel you had outgrown the capabilities of an entire hospital.

The resident who had been on duty all week came in to say good-bye. He stared at Remy with an expression as quizzical as it was tender. I jumped in to reassure him. "She's going to be fine."

"Yes, well, I hope so," he muttered shyly.

"She is. She's going to be totally fine. You guys have done a great job. Now we're going to get over to UCLA and get this thing figured out. We're going to get this cyst taken care of and she'll be fine. Don't you worry about Remy."

He attempted a smile but never rose above forlorn. "Well, God bless you," he said, then headed out. His parting line struck me like a diagnosis.

"What's that supposed to mean?" I said to Lon.

"It didn't mean anything, Heath," Lon answered. But I was already out the door and down the hall, physically pulling at the back of the resident's coat. "Do you know something we don't? Is there some new terrible test result that just came in that I don't know about?"

"No, no . . . nothing."

"She's not going to die, you hear me? She's going to be fine!"

"I'm sorry. I just feel so helpless. I just wish we could have come up with a definite answer for you. I wanted to wish you well, that's all."

"Okay, well, I'm sorry," I said, letting go of his arm. "I just didn't like how it sounded. You know, you've got to watch what you say when you're wearing that coat."

I could hear Remy's room phone ringing from down the hall. It was the call I'd been waiting for: a good friend of ours, Rusty Rodts, who had done his neurosurgical residency at UCLA.

"Heather," he said right up front, "if it were one of my kids, Dr. Peacock is the man I'd want to do it."

"So, I mean, you've seen him do these kinds of things, and, ya know, the kids come out okay and everything?"

"He's the best, absolutely. A truly amazing man. As long as it's not too deep, she should be fine."

"No, it's not too deep. The neurologist said it's not right on the surface, but like, one layer down."

"Okay, good. I'll check in with Dr. Peacock tomorrow, so if you have any questions or just want to talk or anything, call me anytime, okay? This is about the heaviest thing a parent can ever go through," he said, which did not console me in the least. I wanted to cling to the notion that there were much worse things than this. "Middle of the night, whenever—I'm here for you and Lon."

The ambulance arrived at eight-forty-five. We strapped a dozen pink roses into the seat belt up front. I held Remy on my lap in the jump seat in the back. It was like a metallic womb, airtight, with an eerie green fluorescent glow, smelling of rubber and ether and day-old rain. I peered out through the small glass panels in search of a street sign, but the city was a blur, lights and letters smeared in the down-pour, pooly refractions streaking past, swirling, spinning as the ambulance walls closed in around me. It was all I could do not to vomit. "Okay, baby, we're almost there. Everything's going to be just fine." I took deep breaths and stared at an oxygen mask. There was no place for my symptoms. Surely no one would be waiting at the ER gates to ask me how I enjoyed the ride over. We entered through an underground garage, echoey with slick brakes. Lon pulled up right behind us. My aunt Anne was waiting there at my request; she had been married to a man who had worked in those daunting halls for twenty years. I figured she might be able to ease the transition.

We were whisked through Emergency, spelunking laby-rinthine corridors and throughways en route to the east wing and pediatrics; it was as dark and indistinct as everything else I'd seen so far. I peeked into the rooms but found only white mounds and shadow faces bathed in the blue flicker of TV. I sensed Lon drifting away with Remy, but I couldn't fol-low, couldn't move. The hall seemed like an endless dusky mirage. I overheard the ambulance driver: "Well, *my* or-ders say room three-fourteen, and that's where I'm going to release her." I was standing directly in front of room 314. The partition curtain was drawn, concealing the patient, but the family was overwhelmingly visible; there were seven of them, adults and children of all sizes, huddled together, eat-ing crackers and watching a Spanish-language television sta-tion. My ears started to ring. I knew if I had to endure all this and a room full of strangers, I would go mad.

"Well, *we* have instructions to put her in three-forty-seven," the floor nurse said firmly. My aunt was standing right beside her and nodding emphatically.

Lon beckoned me with a silent tilt of his head. I ducked past my aunt and the nurse and the paramedic and joined him at the threshold of a fresh, clean, empty room with one crib and one full-size bed: room 347.

"Grab the bags," I whispered.

We spirited Remy into the room and moved at lightning speed, deploying flower baskets, taping up cards, stocking the sill with foodstuffs (an opened package of graham crackers, two unused jars of pureed pears, a stale biscotti in a Starbucks wrapper and a fresh minibox of Cheerios) and padding the cold steel crib rails — *here we are, home, sweet home* — with a growing menagerie of stuffed animal friends as if our family had been living in that room for generations. I ripped open the complimentary toothbrush packet, spit in the sink to mark it, and closed the door.

It was then I noticed the Day-Glo sign taped to the outside of it: Isolation Room. *Omigod! Was this room just vacated by some highly contagious child who moments ago was whisked away—to where? To ICU? To the coroner?* I turned to see Remy gumming the remote control and ran for my fanny pack, ripping open an alcohol pad and lunging toward the wet plastic germ carrier, assaulting it with frantic strokes. "Hold her, Lon, hold her." I took on the crib edges, the telephone, the gummy vinyl loveseats — anything I could imagine being touched by a human being of any age or size. I flung open the door to find out from the nurse just how serious the contagion might be and heard their discussion coming to a loud and abrupt close: "Well, *our* orders say for her to be in isolation, and that's where I'm going to put her." I realized then that it was us. *It's Remy. We're the ones in isolation.* For once, a hideous label had a perk.

"Hello, welcome," said an older Filipino nurse who found us in our now private room. "I know you must be very tired, so let me just show you a few things quickly. There is a little nightie for her here if you like. And there are diapers and washcloths here. You can change Remy—am I saying it right?"

"Yes, Remy. Like the cognac."

"Ah." She nodded politely. "There is a toothbrush and paste over—oh, I see you already found it, good. Okay then, can you tell me about her meds schedule?"

Five days earlier I wouldn't have had the slightest idea what she was talking about, but today I stated matter-of-factly, "She had her phenobarbital an hour ago—she's on an eight-and-eight schedule—three-point-seven-five cc's each dose. They've been running the acyclovir three times a day—she's due again at midnight; the dose is on her transfer papers. She's been afebrile since one episode of fever yesterday at dinnertime—they've been giving her Tylenol and ibuprofen in rotation as needed, but she hasn't had any today."

Around ten-thirty two residents arrived to check Remy's basic neurological functions: a flashlight in the eyes to make sure that her pupils were small and equal, a reflex test, a Babinski test to see if her big toe curled up upon having the sole of her foot scratched. They held a tongue depressor above her head to see if she could grab it.

"She's very tired, she hasn't slept all day. It's very late," I barbed, as if to explain in advance any shortcomings she might have. But she had none. Remy was under the impression that this was not a medical exam but an audition for *Star Search* and flirted, shrugged, cooed, smiled, waved, maneuvered their sticks like a trained seal and charmed the two doctors mercilessly.

"Range of motion, one hundred percent," they noted matter-of-factly. Lon looked over with a thumbs-up and a grin, but I did not return them. I was no longer wired for small victories. The doctors headed for the door. I rushed them like a crazed Greek heroine. "Tell me she's going to be all right, tell me you can help my little girl!"

"I don't even know what she's doing here," said one resident.

"She has a cyst in her head!"

"Yes, I saw that on the chart," he continued.

"And they can't seem to eliminate the possibility of encephalitis," I added.

"Listen, kids who have encephalitis are very, very ill. This child is extraordinarily healthy—healthiest kid I've seen all month," he said. "Get some rest. You'll meet Dr. Bryson in the morning."

"Who?"

"She's heading up your infectious-disease team," said the second doctor.

"You're really lucky to get to see her," added the other.

"She's, like, the top pediatric herpes specialist in the world."

I tried to picture this woman, the "top pediatric herpes specialist in the world." I decided she looked like that scientist in the Glaxo commercials who works painstakingly at her computer, determined to find some crucial missing piece to her equation, until — "Yes!" she finally exclaims, her small keen eyes lighting up from behind her wire-framed glasses, "there it is." In that moment, in her own little universe, she is transmuted, her geeky brilliance suddenly beguiling. I was nervous about meeting Dr. Bryson, more nervous about that than anything else. She was the specialist of the "unknown" factor, and I was afraid of what she might find.

"C'mon, baby, don't fuss, don't cry. Dr. Bryson wants to see how healthy and happy you are," I said as Lon jiggled Remy unsuccessfully at ten o'clock Friday morning. She and I had been up and all alone together since five. "Please, baby, please stop whining," I begged.

There was a whoosh at the door. "Hello."

I spun around to find a woman in a smart black pantsuit, her arms festooned with chunky folk-art bangles of fuchsia and lime and aquamarine. "I'm Dr. Bryson," she said, with a smile one might find on a travel poster touting Irish hospitality. With an almost imperceptible nod, she instructed the other two members of her team, Dr. Deville and his assistant, to circle around behind me — white coats out of sight — then introduced herself to Lon and settled in on the vinyl loveseat for a chat. A chat, that's what it felt like. But behind her calm green gaze, flecked like tiger's-eye with equal parts warmth and fierce intelligence, I could see her scanning, assessing, conferring silently with her team, watching for telltale signs, and slowly engaging Remy in eyeplay without ever making so much as a move in her direction. "Tell me a little bit about Remy."

"Do you mind if I nurse her while we talk?" I said, knowing it was the only way I could get her to sit still without fussing.

"No, no—that's great. Go right ahead."

I gave her every bit of information I could and then some. "Obviously, I'm not a doctor, but it just seems to me that if that fever spike had been caused by the absence of acyclovir, then she should have spiked a couple times more before the reordered acyclovir could stabilize things. I mean, the spike was at five o'clock. They gave her Tylenol immediately, which means it would have worn off by nine, or, in the case of a really raging temp, by seven or eight, right?"

"Probably."

"Well, they didn't get the acyclovir going again until almost eight o'clock. And obviously, it can't work instantly—it would need some time to get control over the virus, right? I mean, like, what—six hours or something?"

"That's probably a fair assumption."

"So why didn't the fever spike again? If this was a herpes lesion and it's as horrible and fast-moving as everyone keeps saying, then she should have had another fever between eight and say, two A.M. But she didn't. So, anyhow, I know I'm not a doctor, but it just seems to me like it can't be herpes. It just doesn't make sense."

At this point, Remy whipped her mouth off my breast, turned directly toward Dr. Bryson and razzed her. Dr. Bryson razzed back. Remy smiled appreciatively, then returned to her feeding.

"If it is herpes, it's a very atypical case. That's why you're here."

Remy reemerged, cackling at Dr. Bryson, who echoed her throaty flirtations and sent Remy laughing for cover under my shirt. "Let's talk about your delivery. Remy's chart indicates that you have a history of genital herpes—did you have routine cultures leading up to your delivery?"

"With my first child, yes. But this time my doctor told me that the policy had changed or something—that some new guidelines had determined that it was not an effective indicator and they didn't do that anymore," I said. Deep down I had always suspected it was an insurance issue. I braced myself for her response—for the ugly reality that the bean counters had put my daughter at risk—but instead found her looking over at her associates with just a hint of pride.

"Your doctor's right. We changed the guidelines for that last year." From the way she said "we" I got the distinct impression that this very team had personally done the study, formed the conclusions, and issued the global mandate from their very own fax machine to every ob-gyn in the world. Remy popped back up, this time to a full sit on my lap, and reached for the hand-painted ceramic cow dangling from the end of the doctor's glazed-bead necklace.

"But I checked myself every day toward the end," I continued. "I checked right before I went to the hospital. I told the nurse and the doctor to check while I was in labor."

"Well, from what you're telling me it seems highly unlikely that it was passed from you to her at birth," she said, alternating medical factoids with peekaboos. "And even on the outside chance that that did occur, she would have been sick much, much sooner than this. I'm not aware of any case where the virus lay dormant in a baby, then appeared suddenly at nearly eight months."

"So how do you think she could have gotten it?"

"At this point, the herpes virus is present in at least thirty percent of the population worldwide. She could have picked it up from a boxboy or a neighbor or a day-care worker with a cold sore—"

"She's not in day care. She's never been in day care."

"Well, it's out there. Why it chooses to spread to the brain in certain cases, we don't know yet," she said, shifting gears. "I noticed on her chart that you feel she's advanced for her age."

"Well, you know, I mean, I can't say for sure," I backpedaled; my motherly boastings were now being considered as medical analysis. "I mean, I don't know exactly what you'd call advanced."

"She's very advanced," Dr. Bryson said matter-of-factly as Remy suddenly arched backward, lifting her arm up over her head like a water ballerina and making a well-executed swipe at the bright pink pigs clustered at the tips of Dr. Bryson's earrings. I turned and smiled at Lon. *Did you hear that? The leading pediatric herpes specialist in the world feels she's very advanced.* "Well, she does seem to be on the early side of most of the skills in the book," I added modestly.

"Here's what I think we should do. First, let me track down your film—I haven't had a chance to evaluate the MRI yet. Then Dr. Peacock and I will consult. Has he been by yet?"

"No. He's in surgery. They said he's going to look at the scan in between cases—he should be by around three o'clock."

"All right, well, I'll make sure they get me and we can all review our options then. I will tell you this: If it is herpes, we're in great shape. She obviously has no neurological deficit, she's not ill, and we've got the drugs to treat it early."

"Do you really think that's what it is?"

"I need to look at the MRI first. It's not a typical case, that's for sure."

"Have you ever seen a case like this?"

"Yes. Several," she said, reaching for the door.

"Um, I was just wondering," I said, tentatively switching gears. "Are we really in isolation?"

"What? No, of course not. Even if this is a brain lesion, it's not contagious."

"Oh. 'Cause they put us in isolation and now they won't let me take her out of the room and walk around the halls. We're getting a little bit of cabin fever in here."

"Oh, well," she said, reaching for the isolation notice on our door, "I'll just take this off—"

"No!" I said, panic-stricken. "Please—if you take it off, they'll give us a roommate."

She mulled it over for a moment, then looked at me sternly. "You can't have it both ways." She slipped the sign back down in its holder. "You've got a beautiful little girl there. We'll talk more this afternoon." The door swept the infectious-disease team into the corridor, and we were left alone again, this time by choice.

8.

these hands

By 3:00 P.M. all movement had ceased. All motion beyond the reluctant rise and fall of breath was shut down to conserve energy and air. I stared at the sun streaks on the wall beneath the window—even the dust had stopped moving. The O.J. Simpson trial was blasting from a bolted perch near the ceiling, but no one heard a word—not me, not my mom, not Remy, who was curled beside me in a sweaty doze. It was time trapped in a stalled elevator. It was life in limbo.

Then, like a gust, it came. A shift in the room. A warmth, an urgency.

I turned to see an extraordinarily tall man in surgical scrubs. His strides were fluid and without weight, as if his long, trim legs were attached at the hips with suspenders. He had a large manila envelope in his hand and Dr. Bryson at his side.

"Hello," he said, the words made mellifluous by an accent I would later come to know as South African, "I'm Dr. Peacock."

I bolted up off the bed. "Oh, Dr. Peacock," I said and turned away. The TV suddenly seemed obscenely loud. "We've been hearing your name for days," I continued, my back to his face as I shoved my hands under the mattress. "We've been waiting for you," I mumbled, groping the sheets for the remote control—*aha!*

"Where's Papa?" he said brightly, his broad forehead cropped with a green paper cap.

"Oh," I responded, blindly poking every button in search of Off, "he's home with our son. We didn't think you'd be here till much, much later."

"Didn't they tell you three o'clock?"

"Well, yes, but—" *Oh, great, now he thinks Lon is one of those absentee dads.* "Lon wanted to pick him up from school and—" *What is wrong with these fucking controls?* "—we didn't really think you'd be here exactly at—" *Where is the goddamn off button?* "We're really trying to keep things stable for him through all this." Dr. Bryson smiled reassuringly as I—*wham!*—whacked the pesky remote against the wall. The boxy image slurped down to a dot and disappeared. I looked up, the illusion of composure.

"Why don't you tell me a bit about Remy's case?" Dr. Peacock said, wide-eyed.

I hadn't worried too much about this part, expecting that when I was done with my little retelling he would nod as if all was as it should be, given a little cyst of this nature, and verify the findings on the MRI. ". . . I guess they just felt they couldn't be certain about the encephalitis and since they wanted us to see you anyway, they decided to transfer her over here. So here we are," I finished, suddenly less sure.

"Yes, well"—he slipped the film out of the envelope—"I've had a chance to review the MRI. Your daughter has a cystic lesion that I think must be removed."

Yes, I knew that part, okay.

"It is very deep. Extraordinarily deep."

Deep? What? It's not deep, no one ever said it was deep. A thick, tinny buzz swarmed my head, threatening deafness.

"The surgery is extremely difficult," he continued.

Difficult? No, that's not right. You do this every day—this is what you do.

"Why don't you take a look here at her film?" he said, lifting the black plastic photo up to the light.

I tried to stand. *Deep and difficult. The lesion is deep. The surgery is difficult.* "I feel a little, um . . ."

Dr. Bryson stepped in and took my arm. "It's okay, sit down." She kept her hand on my shoulder as we looked at the MRI. My mom stood back, very still, in the corner.

"You see here?" He pointed with his long, slim index finger. "This is the lesion. It's very small—"

"It doesn't look small to me." It looked like a giant jelly-

108

fish hovering over half her brain. *What do "deep" and "difficult" mean? Well, they don't mean good, they don't mean fine. Deep and difficult equal*—

"No, believe me, this is a very small lesion. The difficulty here is the location. It is right up next to the brain stem."

Brain stem, brain stem . . . I scanned my remedial science glossary. *What do I know about brain stems? Something about brain stems and paralysis and*—

"I am almost certain it is benign, probably a—"

"Hamartoma or low-grade astrocytoma," I jumped in, forever trying to beat out the *Jeopardy!* buzzer.

"Yes." He smiled, mildly amused. "There is no edema . . ."

Edema? Edema—swelling, I told myself as I floundered with translations.

"The lesion is completely discrete," he continued.

What the hell does that mean? All I could think of was some bizarre metaphor where the lesion had affairs with the other cells but wasn't flagrant about it. "How are you using the word *discreet?*" I asked.

"Well, no part of the lesion invades the surrounding areas."

Oh, that *discrete.* "It's self-contained," I countered.

"If you prefer," he said, then continued. "A structurally based seizure condition such as hers is extremely hard to control with medication. If the lesion"—he always said "lesion," never "tumor"—"is not removed, she will definitely continue to have seizures. And we don't want that."

"No." *We don't want that.*

"If you were to put these pictures up to ten neurosurgeons, I think they'd agree we're looking almost certainly at a benign growth. I'd say there's an eighty-five-percent certainty of that."

Eighty-five percent. Where have I heard that figure before?

"But of course," Dr. Peacock went on, "the only way to be a hundred percent sure about the nature of a growth is to take it out and have it examined."

So it could be cancer, he's saying it could be cancer, but they won't know until they look.

"I can tell you this," he lilted. "Five years ago I published a paper on my results with this type of surgery. It was the first real data available on cases like these. Out of thirty-five children, we had no fatalities and no morbidities."

Here we go, we have entered the land of "fatalities and morbidities." Okay, think. Fatalities? That's always death. Okay, so he's saying nobody died. So morbidities must be what? Well, something really morbid, something going terribly wrong, something wrong with the brain, serious brain damage—no one was brain-damaged. No one died and no one was brain-damaged? How can that be? What happened to "deep" and "difficult"? I'm missing something. Where is it? What am I missing? What's the catch, goddamn it? Aha! "So kids *have* died since you published the study, right?"

"No," he said, taken aback. "I've never had a bad outcome with a surgery like Remy's."

"And you've done, what? Thousands of them?"

"Oh no. No one's done thousands. I wouldn't even have attempted this surgery ten years ago—it just wasn't done,"

110

he said, inching me closer to an understanding of how well-synchronized their paths were, my daughter's and this man's. "No, I'd say I've done, hmm, seventy-five—maybe a hundred of these. All good outcomes. Saw a boy the other day. Had a situation quite similar to Remy's. I had operated on him as an infant. He's seven now, just as normal as can be."

Normal, normal, why does he keep saying "normal"? My kids aren't normal—they're brilliant and luminous and exceptional. Normal means "ordinary, functioning, average."

"Dr. Bryson and I have discussed the case. She would like some time to eliminate for certain the herpes possibility—after that, I'd like to schedule the surgery."

"If we could do another spinal tap, we could eliminate the herpes right away," Dr. Bryson said. "But now that we've reviewed the scan—"

"A spinal tap with a mass in this location would be extremely risky," Dr. Peacock said, jolting me back to our last night at Santa Monica and the standing emergency order. "Given the proximity to the brain stem, well—" His beeper sounded, and he went on alert. "We won't allow another one to be done." He turned off his beeper. "They're ready for me downstairs. Dr. Bryson will go over the plan with you. I'll stop by tomorrow and we can talk some more. There's a little boy downstairs who needs his shunt replaced."

In an instant he was gone and in his place death hovered like a wraith. I saw now we had come to UCLA not for a cure, but for a verdict. I looked at Remy sleeping, but did not race to her with loving arms. Detachment seemed to be instinctive.

"You're handling this extremely well," said Dr. Bryson. "I'm very impressed with your ability to process this information."

"Oh. Hmm. Thanks," I said, as if someone had just congratulated me on treading water in the middle of the ocean. What other way was there to handle it? I wondered. How did other moms fall apart?

"Here's what we've decided," she said. "We're going to start Remy on a high dose of acyclovir—"

"She's already on that."

"It's not high enough. This will be much stronger. It's a three-week treatment."

"Do these past five days count?"

"No, I'm sorry. The dose just isn't high enough."

"We have to stay here for three weeks?"

"No, I think the plan will be to train you to administer the IVs at home."

"You're kidding."

"I know it sounds scary, but parents do it all the time."

"No. Really," I said, "I'm not very good with my hands. I can't—"

"Listen, don't worry. We'll spend the whole weekend teaching you. We won't release Remy until you feel totally comfortable with the procedure, all right? I promise."

She went on to review their plan of diagnostic attack: They would contact the Santa Monica ER to see if any surplus spinal fluid had been saved for reexamination; they would take fresh samples of blood from me and Remy, compare the antibody levels and observe for changes; and they would take a smear from her hand, which, though dry and nearly healed, might still contain trace evidence. If everything went smoothly, we would have our answer in ten days, and the acyclovir would be canceled or continued, as appropriate.

"But I would still prepare yourself for the surgery," she said. "The chance of it being herpes is very, very slim."

My mom knew not to fill the air with chatter. She rubbed my calves and stared straight ahead, tucking her lips in between her teeth and biting down. The day nurse with the gracious brogue came in to check on us. She took Remy's blood pressure while she slept, then circled round to me, standing over my bed with head tilted, eyes at half-mast, much like the resident had looked at Remy as we prepared to leave Santa Monica.

"Please don't look at me like that. I know what you're thinking — poor woman's going to lose her kid. You probably see it every day — some kid goes off to surgery and never comes back."

"What? No, never. I've never seen a single patient of Dr. Peacock's not leave here smiling."

Deep and difficult. Difficult and deep. The person who has to do the job thinks the job is extremely difficult. Difficult and deep does not equal go home smiling.

The phone interrupted my thoughts. I met the receiver

with Morse code. "He already came. He says the surgery's very difficult. The cyst is extremely deep. We still have to eliminate the herpes. They'll probably do the surgery three weeks from now."

There was a silence on the other end. I imagined that Lon too needed time to process the information. Then he spoke. "Well, we knew that, didn't we? I mean, we never really heard anyone say that it was extremely difficult, or whatever, but I mean, we did know it was brain surgery, right?"

I had had very little strength; now I had less. "I don't want to talk right now."

"I can take Graham next door. I can be up there in —"

"It doesn't matter."

"Well, then maybe I'll just hang out with Graham for the day — we're doing some weeding right now, he's pretty into it. I'll come up after dinner. What do you want me to bring you?"

It was too enervating to form words. Lon said something encouraging and I mumbled "Bye" and hung up. I lay there in a morbid funk, available for Remy's incessant feedings and little else. The depression was so thick I could not imagine it ever lifting. Wrestling with semantics was the only hope I had of digging myself out.

Slowly — word by word, fact by fact — I began to reconcile the pieces of information, stacking them like fine china; so precarious was my logic that I did not dare to move my head as I assembled the thoughts. Hours went by unnoticed. It was dusk when the first glimmer came. I had just stumbled

114

upon an analogy and was pushing it up a metaphorical hill, slowly gathering bulk en route to the top, when Dr. Peacock made a surprise reappearance. It was nearly six o'clock.

He walked past my bed, patting me gently on the thigh—a father checking in on a teenage daughter after her first big breakup. "So, Mom, how're you doing?"

I didn't have the energy to sit up. I lifted no more than my eyes to meet his. "I'm working on an analogy."

"Good, I love analogies."

"Okay, well, I'm not really a skier or anything, but if we were skiing, how would we rate this? Would you say this surgery would be a black diamond run?"

"Oh yes. It's definitely a black diamond run."

"Oh."

"But it's a black diamond run first thing in the morning, no moguls."

This is the problem with devising analogies that are out of your field of expertise: If someone decides to run with it, you're lost—kind of like saying *"Bonjour"* to a Frenchman when that's the full extent of your French. *Well, the whole fresh-start concept is almost universally good, so "first thing in the morning" must be a plus. Moguls? What are moguls? Bumps. Bumps of any kind are, as a rule, bad. So "no moguls" must be good.*

"Some of the kids I work on, their brains are just a mass of scars and mistakes and dead tissue, far more difficult than little Remy. She'll be fresh powder all the way."

Fresh powder, fresh powder? . . . It's light, it's fluffy. Good. "Fresh powder" is good.

115

"Okay, so it's a black diamond run, but you're a world-class skier, right?"

"Well . . ." He blushed.

"Well, you are. And a world-class skier should be able to get down the hill, especially on fresh powder, right? I mean, that's what world-class skiers do, right?"

"Yes, that's what we do."

"I mean, I know you're human. I know you can fall, you can hit those little orange markers. There are, you know, other factors, like weather and things, but it would not be unreasonable for us to expect you to make it down the hill alive."

"Listen, I think we're going to have a very good outcome with Remy. There's a boy right next door—flew in last week from Venezuela. Yesterday I took out half his brain. Today he's sitting up eating ice cream."

"Wow," I said flatly. I didn't know why a boy would have to have half his brain taken out—I didn't want to know. What struck me most was that we had just been reseeded on the scale of "How would you rank this, as medical crises go?" and the only person to compare us to as a gesture of consolation was a boy from another continent who now had half a brain. I changed the subject. "So what do you think about the herpes thing—you think that's really a possibility?"

"I don't think so. I work on kids every day with encephalitic masses—this is not that."

"So you don't think we should do the treatment?"

"No, I think you should. The medication has no real downside, other than the hassle for the parents. On the off chance I'm wrong, it's worth it. Little Remy is my patient, she is my number-one concern. Your inconvenience is secondary to me. If the treatment would get her out of the surgery, I'd be euphoric."

Oh, great, so the surgeon would be euphoric not to have to perform the surgery. "But we should prepare for the surgery?"

"Definitely. As soon as you've finished with the acyclovir, you call me. We'll set a date."

"You're not worried about waiting three weeks?"

"No, that should be fine. I wouldn't let it go much longer, though. Get some rest."

He patted my forearm gently and bid me good night. It was then I began thinking about his hands. They were the color of pale honey, his skin stretched like translucent suede over a frame more arachnidlike than human. The way he moved each joint, each digit—such floaty precision—as if each skeletal millimeter was capable of autonomous tasks. Even through my despair, I was distracted by their grace, half expecting, each time I looked back, to find spun gold in their webs. *We are here for a reason.* It was not by coincidence that this man who would become a surgeon was given these fine, liquid hands. *He probably learned to tie his shoes at three.* It was not by chance that he had come into the world with both the intelligence and the opportunity to excel in his field. *Did he bring home wounded birds from school and mend their wings?* It was not a fluke

9.

someone to watch over me

They began like electric shock, these mornings, these days, as Remy would cry out and I would jump, my brain like a Brillo pad soaked in glue as I comprehended anew the four tight walls of graying paint, the jaundiced fluorescence, the tedious hiss, the aching hollow of unknowable absolutes. They were the loneliest dawns imaginable.

At five-forty-five Saturday morning, a man entered our room: a stranger with a shaved head and tattoos and low-riding chinos. If I had passed him on the street in Venice, I would have crossed to the other side. If he had hung around my street too long, I might have called the police. The moment he cleared the doorway Remy lit up like a Glow Stick. "Hello, bebé. How are you today, beautiful girl?" She flapped her arms, he leaned in toward her high-chair tray. "You love those li'l Cheerios, don't you? How many you have today—let's count them, heh? *Uno, dos, tres . . .*" She stared enrapt at his strange words.

"You mind if I run and get some coffee real quick?" I asked.

"No, go 'head, I watch her. Go to the west wing kitchen—it's fresher," said the janitor, dumping our soiled diapers and lining the trash can with a new bag.

For the next four hours, Remy and I paced the same five feet of stupefying floor until it was all I could do not to scream. If I had, a nurse would have looked in and soon thereafter some notation would have been made on Remy's chart about the relative instability of the mother. The information would then have been passed along from shift to shift with Remy's meds schedule and vitals and urine output, so that a tantrum at eight o'clock in the morning would cause a nurse at eight at night to approach me with condescending caution.

An antiseptic resident came by to interview me about my maternity history; apparently, there was a need—medical, ethical, I wasn't sure what—to determine if this whole thing was somehow my fault. I told her that heinous sinus pain had led me to take Sudafed on several occasions in the first trimester. That I'd allowed myself one cup of coffee a morning, and one glass of wine a week from the sixth month on.

"Oh," I said, just then remembering, "and I did have a

120

few high blood-sugar readings near the third trimester—you know, that maternal diabetes everyone gets. I was really borderline, though." I thought back to that time, before my daughter even existed. Twice a day I had pricked my finger, squeezing the tip till the blood pooled up. Graham was fascinated, curling up at the foot of my bed each morning as I laid out the reactor strips and the pricker and the digitized monitor.

"Can I taste it?" he had asked. "Can I taste the blood?" he'd said each morning, each night.

"No," I'd said, certain that that's what a grown-up is supposed to say. It occurred to me that if he went on to become some sort of satanic ritualist, this lapse in parental judgment would be revealed in a trial of some sort and pinpointed by an expert as the root of his errant ways. But after a while, I didn't care. I was so sluggish and cumbersome, I longed to be the cause of one of his generous smiles. "Okay, just this once," I'd said, and lifted my fingertip to his lips. But I did not tell the young resident about that.

Remy's head sprang a leak. It was decided she needed a PICC line, a peripherally inserted central catheter, which is established by inserting a tube into a vein in the foot, threading it through the calf, up through the thigh, and on into a nice, juicy central vein in the groin. Unfortunately, Remy's skin was too taut or her veins too churlish—something—and they were unable to worm the line up much past mid-calf. "It might last, it might not," they said upon their return from the procedure room. "We'll just have to wait and see."

To hold the line secure, they taped a splint from the tip of Remy's toes up past the bend in her left knee, restricting all movement below the hip. Until that point, the biggest thrill of her day was being able to pull herself up to standing—she had just figured out how to do it and now wanted to repeat the task four or five thousand times, preferably to a cheering crowd. She knew not from splints. If I sat her in the crib, she would grab hold of the steel rails and face-plant right into them not once, but repeatedly, clambering to right herself even while her little fleshy nose was still smashed into the metal. If I put her on the bed or the chair beside me, she would plow forward, collapsing in much the same fashion. But neither pain nor failure would deter her. I watched her rise, again and again—an athlete in training, hell-bent on mastering the skill at hand. When her fierceness of will proved insufficient, she decided to take on the obstacle itself, tugging at the thick, restrictive leg board and groping so furiously at the tubing I thought she might peel a seam straight down her calf. I pinned her arms to her sides and pressed down on her like keepsake flowers. She arched and jerked and kamikazed herself toward the floor. Finally, hours into our workout, she knocked herself into a state of collapse.

"Oh, good, she's sleeping," the night nurse said the minute I covered her with a blanket. "Let's get you started with your IV procedures. Here, hold this," she said, handing me a sealed vial.

She went on to demonstrate how to uncap the needle, how

to prep the surface of the medication bottle with Betadine and alcohol rubs—"thirty seconds of firm wiping motions each"—how to insert the needle and slowly draw back the fluid to the indicated cc line. I thought about Graham and how when he was an infant I lacerated his little fingers not once but three times trying to operate the baby nail clippers. Lon took over all manicures, pedicures and haircuts shortly thereafter.

"When the syringe is full, you tap it several times firmly to loosen any air bubbles. That's really important. Then push it in just a hair to release the air out from the tip."

I scrunched up my face and flicked emphatically at the plastic. I checked closely and saw nothing. I checked again. "There, how's that?" I said proudly.

She eyed the syringe and grew somber. "Uh-uh. No. Look. You've got a big air bubble right here."

"What? Where?" The nurse tapped hard on the syringe. A fat, lazy sphere floated up through the fluid. "But I didn't even see that. I thought it was clear. I really checked. What would have happened if I had used that syringe?"

"Well, you don't want air bubbles in the bloodstream, let's just say that, okay?"

Scuba diving came to mind—*air bubbles, something about air bubbles in the body, in the lungs, something about imploding.* My life was suddenly one big daredevil-sports analogy.

Remy was now breastfeeding eight, ten, twelve times a day. Since her seizure, she'd gained two pounds and I'd lost eight.

"There's blueberry . . . ," my mom said, rifling through a now day-old bag of gourmet take-out muffins.

"I'm not really hungry."

"There's something orangey — maybe pumpkin."

"Maybe later."

"Here. How 'bout a half a poppy-seed?"

"Just leave it, okay?"

She set the bag aside and walked toward the sink, looking into the mirror and away from me as she spoke. "You know, I just finished reading about an amazing study. It was on prayer and healing." I rolled my eyes discreetly but did not tell her to stop. "They took two groups of heart patients, both equally sick. Then they assigned people to pray for half of them. They picked all different kinds of people, from every kind of religion, and just asked them to pray in whatever way worked for them, to pray for these particular heart patients. And the results were phenomenal. The people who were being prayed for, without exception, healed faster and more completely than the group who was not being prayed for."

"Well, yeah, I'm sure. Just knowing all these people were rooting for you, the whole power-of-positive-thinking thing — it's not really that surprising."

"No," she said, this time right to me. "That's just it. They didn't know. The patients weren't told. They had no idea that anyone was praying for them. It was totally anonymous, and still, every single one of the prayer recipients got better."

"Oh," I said, and started looking around. "Did you say there was pumpkin?"

*　　*　　*

It was late and the room was dark when the knock came and the door opened and I smiled. "You're still here?" I said.

"Yeah, just finishing up," the janitor said, making his nightly rounds. The last time I had seen him was at six that morning. It was now after nine o'clock.

"That's a long day."

"I get a day off tomorrow."

"Oh," I said, and I flashed on how the morning would be without him. "She'll miss you."

"I'll be back on Monday. You still be here?" he asked as he dumped the soiled linens into a bigger bin.

"I think so."

"She gonna be okay?"

"I don't know," I said for the very first time. "I hope so."

"I have a little talk with the man upstairs," he said, backing his cart into the hall.

"Enjoy your day off."

"I will. G'night."

" 'Night."

"I have some brochures here about the diaphragm," the doctor had said.

"No," I interrupted. "I don't want a diaphragm. I want to have my tubes tied. That's what you call it, right?"

"Well, yes," he said, struggling to maintain his composure, "but I think you're a little young to be making such a permanent decision. I'm sure later on, when you're married, you'll change—"

"I'm not having kids. I don't like kids. I feel no urge to dress them up and have some little thing to cuddle. I don't even like dogs—hate them, in fact. No," I continued, certain that at fifteen years of age I was quite capable of making adult decisions, "I'm not going to change my mind. I have things to do—big things to do—and I can tell you absolutely, positively, I am never going to have kids."

He looked over at Suzie to see if she might shed any light on the situation. Suzie was my very best friend throughout most of high school. We were inseparable. When I decided I was ready for sex—not specifically, but in theory—it was Suzie who drove me to the gynecologist, and it was Suzie who was standing in the exam room, thinking long term. "How about a diaphragm for now?"

Toward the end of our senior year, I found some people to appreciate my diaphragm and Suzie found god. Her neighbor's thirteen-year-old son had hung himself in the garage and she was looking for answers. I didn't understand why she would look to god for them; it seemed quite obvious that if there was a god, he would not have allowed a thirteen-year-old boy to hang himself.

"You would be third," she told me one night as we sprawled on our backs staring up at the cottage-cheese ceiling. "God is first, my husband will be second, and you will probably be third."

I sat up very straight to make the following point. "Well, I'm sorry to disappoint you, but I don't want to be best friends with someone who puts me third. If I can't be the most important thing in your life anymore, then you can certainly not be the most important thing in mine." After that, we were separable.

At eight o'clock Sunday morning, Suzie arrived at UCLA with coffee, scones and a masseur. He wheeled in a strange, kneel-down-and-flop-forward chairlike contraption and proceeded to knead my scalp and my ears and my neck and my arms and my shoulders and my spine and my scrunched-up sacroiliac, then, in a hush, stepped away to meditate over my sleeping daughter, leaving me, face to the floor, thinking, *Hey, what about my feet?* I must have thought it really loudly because Suzie jumped right up. "What is it? What do you need?" and pressed her firm sculptor's fingers into my tired soles for another half an hour.

"There are angels here," a man's voice said. Suzie and I turned toward the masseur, who was now standing in the doorway, fold-up chair in hand. "This room is one of the most inspiring places I've ever been in. Thank you."

I turned to examine this inspiring place, the muddied salmon walls, the sticky puke-colored loveseats, the daylight filtered through dust-caked industrial glass. "I know what he means. I can feel it. I can feel the angels here. It's really pretty amazing how quickly your thinking changes—" I said, then stopped. We were adult friends now; I asked Suzie about work, she asked me about the kids. We had tried on occasion to scratch the surface of religion, but we were always worlds apart; eventually we just stopped trying. "But then, you already know all about this stuff," I said.

"Not really. No," she said. "I haven't been to church in years."

Remy cried out. I reached in to get her and found my hand skimming a puddle of pure, cool liquid. A specialist from the pediatric ICU was called in to evaluate her IV. I watched her firm pinto-colored hands examining Remy's fleshy white calf. "This one's already shot. It won't even take the sedative she'll need to start up a new one."

"Well, are you going to try the other leg or what? 'Cause, I mean, if you can do it without this leg splint, I would really appreciate it," I said to the woman, who was looking at me as if my appreciation was not high on her list of concerns. "It's just that the splint makes everything so much harder on her."

"I don't think we'll have any more luck with the other leg. She's got good neck veins. I'll use one of those," she said, then looked off at some unspecified point near the ceiling. I could see her mind working, rifling through case histories, factoring in all the variables—age, weight, dosage, illness, likely home environment—all in a nanosecond. "Okay, I'll butterfly the neck, we'll sedate directly into the jugular, then we'll thread the cath from there. Let me warn you now. This line goes directly into the central artery in the chest—any germs, dust, household dirt, whatever—could introduce an infection that could spread quite rapidly. You'll be administering the IVs yourself?"

"Yes."

"Well, just be *extremely* careful about cleanliness, okay?

The risk of infection is really the most serious concern we have when we send people home with these lines."

Christine was scheduled for the 7:00 P.M. shift. "Here," I said, thrusting my daughter into her arms and heading for the door. On the night Remy was born, it was Christine who had gotten her to stop screaming inconsolably, Christine who had stood like a mother hen outside the nursery window as they weighed her and bathed her and pricked her heel for PKU. "I've gotta get out of here," I barked, and Christine nodded to me to go, already entrancing Remy with a nursery rhyme in French.

I had not left the floor since the ambulance driver had escorted us up through the back entrance four days earlier. I had no idea where I was, where the elevators were. I didn't care. I was free—for a few moments, anyway—free. I found a set of back stairs and flew down them, surprised at how winded I grew after only three flights. I spilled out onto a courtyard that led nowhere, then circled back to the cafeteria, which was closed. No obstacle annoyed me—I had no game plan. I was out, I was walking amongst the living. I came across a cavern filled with vending machines and tables. It was a Sunday night, but the place was packed. *Who are all these people? Students? They must be students.* Hundreds of them, huddled in study groups and hunkered down alone, in corners, in chairs, in hallways, eating their microwave cheeseburgers and thinking their microscopic thoughts. The building was filled with the sick and

129

the maimed and the dying, but all around was a volu-
minous buzz of hope — white-hot, electric hope! — as these
fine young minds sucked up symptoms and Gatorade, ready-
ing themselves to spill out onto these floors like kids at an
egg hunt.

It was then I felt certain that all good is possible, nothing
is hopeless, no cure is out of reach, and the unfathomable
should be lustily and wholeheartedly embraced.

Remy was as charged up as I was that night. She had
rediscovered the freedom of a splintless leg and was thrilled
to be rocking the crib rails. Her arterial line (a three-inch-
long white plastic tube with a pale blue tip sprouting out
from her jugular) flopped around on the side of her neck
like the coil antenna of a child's pull toy. We laughed and
sang and played. *There are angels here.* I could feel them
in my laugh, in Remy's smile. I twirled her around the
room, and the words flew out from the depths of my soul
just as they had the day she was born. "How did I get so
lucky? How did I get so lucky to have you, my beautiful
angel?"

By ten-thirty, I had grown tired of the lovefest. I needed
to do my homework, but Remy would have no part of it. I
put her down, she popped right back up. I closed the curtain
between the two of us and began to read. *"When connecting
the entry port to the catheter plug, remember to . . ."* A giggle
stole me away. Remy had moved to the end of the crib and
was now pulling the curtain back in a newfound game of

peekaboo. I responded with impressive threats like "If you don't go to sleep this minute, I'm going to have them put the splint back on—don't think I won't do it."

It was midnight before we slept, but I will remember those Sunday-night hours of sleeplessness as some of the most delicious and crystalline moments of love I have ever experienced.

10.

david

"How will he find us?" I asked.

"He has your address," the hospital administrator assured me.

"And you're telling me he'll be there on time."

"He'll be there."

"What if he can't find the house? What if they send the wrong stuff? I'm sorry, I don't like this whole plan."

The plan was this: We would leave UCLA and somehow, between when we arrived home and when Remy's next dose of intravenous acyclovir was scheduled, a delivery of all the necessary medicine and IV supplies would be made to our home. Then, at 6:00 P.M., exactly at the time when the next dose was due, a nurse would walk in the door to watch me do something I had practiced the various steps for but had yet to do from start to finish. It was all too much. Too many variables, too many logistics, too little margin for error—it was just too great a leap.

"Don't worry," the hospital administrator said over and over again. "He'll find you."

We were officially released at ten o'clock on Monday morning, immediately after one of Remy's three daily acyclovir doses. That meant we had eight hours to get home, settle in, scour and prep her room, and be ready to administer the next dose of acyclovir. At two, we were still not home. Half of the eight hours—of *my* precious eight hours—were spent sitting in a hospital room we no longer needed, while someone wrote up a prescription for phenobarbital and some ill-defined verifications were made with the home health care people. This did not instill in me a general feeling of calm.

"Oh, good, you're still here," a nurse I'd never seen before said as she stepped over our packed bags. "I need to see you do a dressing change before you go." I tried to get out of it, but not very hard. I figured if this was something I was going to have to do at home, I'd better try it once with someone watching.

We pinned Remy down on her back. Lon held her head down flat; it took almost his entire body weight to keep her neck still as she jerked and screamed. My fingers approached the site like timid children as I pinched back the corner of the thin cellulose bandage—spurt, gurgle—her jugular started to gush, thick purple bursts of warm blood pouring out for what seemed like eternity.

"The sites bleed like this when they're fresh, sometimes," said the nurse blandly.

"Are you sure? Are you sure I'm doing it right? This is a lot of blood!" I screamed, my brow knit like day-old gum.

Unlike the IV process, there was no distance in a dressing change. I had to do things to her directly, my hands on her neck, which was being twisted round and presented to me by means of extreme pressure to her head. I steadied my fingers on a presoaked Betadine swab and pointed the rust-tipped swab toward the site. It was the first time I had seen this gash in my baby girl—seen the tube jutting out like some alien worm secured to her skin with menacing black cilia. Foul air rose up from my stomach to my throat. I pressed the Betadine into the stitches, swiping it around in firm outward circles, forcing germs away from the site. This, while Remy writhed like a fish in a net. "Please, Rem, please stop screaming, please, baby, I'm doing the best I can." Each lurch cranked fresh blood from the wound.

The manual called for six swabs of Betadine, six swabs of alcohol, a layer of fresh antibiotic ointment—not too much, not too little—a fresh square of gauze, and finally, a microthin translucent adhesive patch that clung to itself so mercilessly that getting it out of the wrapper and onto Remy was like Lucy pulling taffy. "Goddamn it!" I screamed. The nurse rolled her eyes. Remy kicked me in the chest. Lon breathed loudly to remind me to. I wanted to kill someone; I didn't much care who. "There," I said, finally getting the bandage smooth and in place.

"Good," said the nurse, checking off an item on her list. "Now, you'll need to do this every other day until she has the line removed, all right?"

It was in this moment that I thought about money and why it was occasionally useful. *I don't care what it costs, I don't care whom we have to bring in, but I am never doing another dressing change as long as I live.*

A resident entered unannounced. "I want to double-check this site before she leaves."

"What?" I said, in barely a whisper.

"Can you please strip down the dressing?"

"I just did it. I just finished it."

"I heard there was some bleeding. I need to see the site."

"There's no way. I'm done. I am not doing it again."

"I don't think it's a good idea to release her without checking it."

"We were released four hours ago!" I screamed.

"Well, I can't let her leave without checking it."

"Fine. If you want to check the site, *you* strip it down and *you* redo it. I've had it. I've done my dressing change." I did not look over to see Lon's eyes as I stormed out of the room, leaving him to hold her down as the entire process was repeated. I was trembling and furious, red hot and seething—I had reached my boiling point and then some.

I raged toward the pediatrics kitchen, battering open the door and almost knocking down the man standing behind it. "Oh, sorry, I'm sorry. I'm just totally losing it. Sorry," I mumbled.

"I understand," he said. He had sandy hair combed back wet, and deep blue eyes made watery by time. He was Lon ten years from now. I had seen him arrive earlier that day in his khaki shorts and worn green T-shirt, his belly grown soft from life's obligations. He was pushing a girl Graham's age down the hall in a stroller.

"It's just all these fucking details, the IVs and the bandages and the blood draws and the medicine—you know, as if it's not enough you have to deal with the idea of brain surgery, you've got all this stuff, too."

"I remember the first time they took blood from my daughter. I almost fainted. Now we shoot stuff straight into her chest at home." My whimpering was abruptly doused. "When are you having the surgery?" he continued.

"Probably a few weeks from now. They're not exactly sure."

"Well, the brain patients do really well here. The doctors are the best."

"Yeah? Is that what your daughter is here for?"

"No. Her heart. She's having surgery tomorrow. It'll be her fifth one. We almost lost her after the third one. The fourth time she was in ICU for twenty-six days—that's hard, there's just nothing you can do. My wife and I took turns waiting it out."

"You live nearby?"

"No. Sacramento. We were medevacked down here the last two times. It was really touch and go."

"So your wife's there now?"

"Well, we have three other kids—a boy, fourteen, a girl, twelve, and another boy, six. The older kids are pretty used to it by now—they have their own lives—but the six-year-old, that's who it's hardest on. He's kind of gotten lost in the shuffle. And they're buddies, you know? That's his playmate. Every time we come down here he asks, 'Is she going to die? Is my sister going to die this time?' " I imagined him, this six-year-old boy, bottomed out on a teeter-totter. "The surgery tomorrow is the riskiest one yet. My wife and I have to talk about it each time—what we should do, you know, if she doesn't make it. If I'm with her when it's happening, things she wants me to whisper in her ear."

"I can't imagine," I said, when nothing would have been fine.

"You get used to it, I guess. We've been doing this for almost five years now—just praying for one of the surgeries to take."

"What do they say?"

"They don't know. They're the best in the world and they don't know. We say a lot of prayers."

"It's starting to seem like that's how things work around here."

"Hey," he brightened, reciting a lilty catchphrase undoubtedly picked up at some sort of support meeting. "When you're down this low, there's nowhere to look but up."

"Yep," I said, then thought about the time; the last I had

checked, it was nearly three o'clock. "I should be getting back. I'm Heather."

"David."

"Good luck to you tomorrow," I said.

"Thanks."

I headed back to Remy's room, my head pounding. *Good luck to you? What is that? Good luck to you? That's a kiss-off to an unwelcome solicitor. Good luck to you? No. No!* I thought as I rounded back to our room and saw Lon and Remy, rebandaged and ready to go.

"All set?" Lon asked.

"No. Wait." I ran back to the kitchen. It was locked up tight. I looked up and down the halls. No khaki shorts. No worn brown loafers on bare feet. I returned to the room, unsettled. Remy whipped her arms around in cheerleader circles and stretched my way. I scooped her up, wiping her tears and nose with my shirt. "Okay, my big brave girl," I said, then added reluctantly, "Let's go."

We headed down the hall. I kissed her fat pink cheek, looking over her shoulder, right then left, inspecting every room. In each bed was a sick child. In each room was a mom or a dad and the heavy air of uncertainty. But no David. We passed a cabal of residents outside a door. I looked in, but still no—not them, not there.

A girl's murmury laugh inched out into the hall and I doubled back. In the playroom there was a preschooler, her spindly legs unable to stretch the seams of her pink flowered leggings. She turned to reach for a block. There was a breathing tube imbedded in her nostrils. It hung down against her

138

pale gray skin and connected to a small metal tank. *Where is your father, sweet angel? Where is your daddy?* A hand leaned in, adding a block to her stack. I caught his eye from the doorway.

"David?"

He looked up, confused, called back from some distant thought. His eyes welled behind his wire-rimmed glasses.

"God bless you," I said, crack-voiced and weakening. "God bless you both."

Remy swatted the string on her Minnie Mouse balloon and thwacked it against my cheek. We headed for the elevators. "Okay, baby," I whispered, waiting for the doors to close to raise my voice. "Mama and Rem are going home!"

11.

home

The corporate universe is not without its charms. Without it, I would never have met Lon. I would never have met my friend Thérèse (at whose wedding I wept so profusely), or Thérèse's brother Rob (who would go on to become Graham's godfather), or Thérèse's brother-in-law Rusty (then a neurosurgical intern at UCLA).

And I would never have been able to amass the nest egg of stock and profit sharing that enabled Lon and me to buy a house. I still remember the one we fell in love with. It had two stories with three big bedrooms and a gourmet kitchen and a separate dining room and a big backyard with a toolshed just waiting to be a fort. This house was by far the most house we could afford. We stood in the bathroom of the master suite, leaning against the his and her sinks, my face all honeymooney full of "well?"

"If we get this house," Lon said with prescient calm, "you cannot quit your job. Not for a long, long time."

I wondered at the time if he was speaking specifically to the fact that the politics of business were eating me alive and he wanted me to save myself, or of something loftier, like the price of materialism being one's soul. Lon was a navy officer's son, never poor enough to be enamored of money, never rich enough to be accustomed to it. He was practical to a fault. Most likely what he meant was that this was a two-paycheck house and he wasn't going to get stuck with all that mortgage when I decided to stay home with our kids. I'll never know for sure, but we opted instead for a house half the size and moved in on Valentine's Day.

I left the advertising business six months later. To subsidize this leap, I went on a game show, won $23,000, and began a course load of UCLA extension classes with a plan to transition to a home-based writing career. If I had a picture of myself as a writer, it was as a writer of books: a writer of books who leaned against an old wooden desk and encouraged those coming up in the world with a passion to speak their minds. But I could not write a book. Not then, not yet. A writer of books was one who attempted to explain Life's Great Truths—or should be—and I suspected that my precocious certainties would not hold up to the unwieldy grays of Real Life. I decided to write screenplays instead.

I had always loved the movies. When I was seven years old, I remember convincing our East Indian exchange student/baby-sitter that I was allowed to attend matinees on my own. He gave me twenty dollars from the petty cash fund and dropped me off in front of the Village Theatre in Westwood, where I stood on my tiptoes to buy a ticket. I remember scrunching down in the warm velvet seats in the dark, near-empty theater and thinking, *Aaahhh*. It was the second-best feeling in the world.

The first was reading, which I fell in love with at the age of three. One day, as the story goes, I had tagged along for Michael's phonics tutorial, when, seeing him struggle, I picked up a book off the table and said, "Here, Michael, like this . . ." and proceeded to read it aloud to him. After that, I couldn't get enough. Heaven on earth was a trip to the library on Friday afternoons, where I would stuff my book bag to the limit and spread out on my parents' king-size bed surrounded by pillows that smelled like both of them together, reading till our live-in maid told me it was time for bed, and even then I hid with a flashlight and read some more. Shortly after the big house was sold and I moved to the house on the hill overlooking the dark, snarling canyon—the same kind that Charles Manson's "family" had crept through to slice open Sharon Tate and her baby and the LaBiancas—I stopped reading altogether.

By the time Graham was born, I had written five screenplays, all unsold—for the most part, unread. There was the occasional opened door at the entrance of which scripts were stacked like pillars to remind you of your insignificance. It

142

occurred to me that people who wanted to succeed at this would look at those foreboding stacks and wonder, "What do I have to do to get on top?" But all I could think was, *What am I doing here?* It was a question there would be no point in asking, because inside those slick black rooms, words lost all meaning. By the time they crossed the two-ton coffee tables they would dissipate like a vapor. It was as if they were somehow encoded. I sensed once or twice that I might be offered the code if only I gave the right answers, but I did not.

Lon fled the corporate world as well. He was struggling to get freelance work at home, and our checking account hovered around figures I usually associated with the gas bill. But there would be no turning back. Each minute of each day I knew that our son had the rare privilege of growing up in a house where the pillows smell like mom and dad, where children's brief years are sacred and irreplaceable, and where no one tenses up when the phone rings at 5:00 P.M. because there is no such thing as being *stuck* at the office.

That was the snapshot I held in my mind. It was lovely, reassuring. But it was not the whole truth.

I had envisioned home as freedom. Home was meant to be the slow, warm pace of life in nature, where souls can burrow in the ground like bulbs in winter, slowly taking what they need to grow and thrive, gathering steam, staying safe and warm and steeped in pure soil until they are fully realized, then pushing up and out, strong and bright and wholly individual. And for a while, it was just that.

But the vision had grown murky. As Graham neared two, my days were spent staring off past the high point of a rising swing, no longer sure why I was there. *Am I a dedicated mother, or just a failed writer?* My evenings were spent dreaming of being productive. But I was too exhausted to do anything more than collapse in front of the TV lost in a blur of sitcoms that left me restless and dissatisfied. I would pour a glass of wine —*just one, one's okay* — just enough to make the dull comedy palatable and the gnawing urge to achieve lie still. But then I would hate myself for the wine and the fruitlessness of my few spare hours. I could always hear Lon in the background, making his busy little noises, folding laundry, paying bills, filling the juice-pop trays — so functional. I resented his usefulness and wished he would just once sit down with a big fat beer and watch *Roseanne* like every other husband in America. *Quiet desperation.* My nights were spent sleeping as hard as I could, but it was never long enough.

I tried to imagine the big picture — The Really Big Picture — and could not believe that this was the plan. If women existed for no greater purpose than the birthing and rearing of children, I wondered, then what kind of a cruel joke was it to give us any talent at all beyond meal preparation, which clearly I did not have? Each and every night, as the clock pushed past five, I would look up, startled, as if just remembering the birthday of some distant cousin I'd forgotten to send a card to, and say, "Oh god. Dinner."

But someone knew enough to give me Lon, who was perfectly content eating yogurt and bananas and peanut-butter toast at any of the three meals. "Look, Mom made us Crispix for dinner," he would say to Graham with a surprise-party enthusiasm that forced me to smile. But even he could not restore me. Not then. Not as my brother lay dying, and my mother lay weeping, and I lay pining for things I wouldn't allow myself to want. *If I could just . . .* It was very noisy in my head. Sometimes it got so loud, I feared I might quite literally die from it—just keel right over in the sandbox, digging in the shadow of our 1,200-square-foot home.

We had been back from the hospital for twelve minutes when the home health care delivery van arrived. I signed my name on a clipboard form and watched a young man in a white uniform deposit two enormous boxes on our living-room floor.

Inside there were dozens of Ziploc bags, each filled with shrink-wrapped plugs and caps, blue ones and red ones and green ones—scores of them—and hundreds upon hundreds of sterile plastic syringes. There were vials of various solutions and a stack of dressing kits. There was surgical soap, medical tape, and an ominous disposal container marked with a skull and crossbones. There were three hand-grenade-like balloons made of semihard plastic encasing mustard-yellow bags that appeared to be deflatable. They were labeled "Remy Davis: Acyclovir."

"Wow," Lon exclaimed, emerging from the yard with Remy in the backpack.

"I've never seen any of this stuff before," I informed him.

"What? You're kidding."

"No." Not a single item in either of the two boxes matched any plug or tube or syringe I'd practiced with for the past three days. They were vaguely similar, but they were not the same. I lay down on the couch and shut my eyes, assessing my dilemma with a desperate calm. I heard a cabinet door open, a bag unzip. I recognized the sounds but did not believe my ears. *Click, whir, cha-ching. Click, whir, cha-ching.*

"I'm glad you find this so amusing," I said, staring directly into the lens of Lon's Nikon with an evil eye.

"It's for the baby book—you'll be glad to have these shots later."

"I don't think so."

He repositioned a bag of Betadine swabs atop the hazardous waste bucket, then scooted them both in a grouping beside the syringes. I could see him back in art school, painting nudes and bowls of fruit. *Click, whir, cha-ching.*

"I think that's enough." *Click, whir, cha-ching.* Graham ran into the house from a neighbor's—"Hi, Mom. Oh, wow"—and dove at the boxes like they were the treasure chest at the dentist's office.

"Stop!" I pounced. "Don't touch anything. If you touch any of it, you could make Remy very, very sick. Do you understand?" Graham stepped away, horrified. I took a breath and began again. "I'm sorry, I didn't mean to scare

146

you, but it's really important to keep everything clean and sterile—you know what *sterile* means? It means it's never been touched by anything, so you know there's no germs on it, okay? Here, look," I said, opening one of the needleless syringes. "Here, this one is for you. This is what I'll be using to push the medicine and stuff into the tube Remy has in her neck. Why don't we put your name on this one, okay?"

"Can I have one of those things, too?"

"Sure, it looks like we've got plenty. Why don't you take one of the blue ones and the green ones—and here, look—you can have a whole roll of this tape." His eyes lit up like I'd given him a block of gold.

"Come here," I said, longing, after a week without his touch, to burrow my nose into his sweet boyish musk.

The doorbell rang at 5:59 P.M. "Don't answer it," I snapped. Seconds later a burly, poker-faced Persian woman was standing beside me, making demands. "Let's wash," she said. I led her into the bathroom, skulking and pleading my case: "But . . . but . . ." I told the nurse about the strange new IV parts and how nothing was the same as I had learned it.

"Variations on a theme," she responded, unmoved. "Let's prep."

Lon and I had fashioned a makeshift work surface out of an ironing board and a glass shelf and set it up next to Remy's crib. I approached it like a gangplank. "Okay, well, uh . . . first, I need to draw my syringes."

"Two saline and one heparin. One cc each, please. You'll

flush the line with saline before administering the IV, then flush once each with saline and heparin after each dose. All right, let's get the baby. I'll watch you start the IV."

"What? No. I can't. I told you. This is all different from the stuff I learned with."

"This system is much easier. The syringes are needleless, the lines are preprimed, the medicine bags are portable—all much better for home use. It's six-seventeen. We need to move along."

Lon held Remy in his lap with a book. I knelt just outside her field of peripheral vision, sliding my hands in from behind. The first thing I needed to do was remove the cap from the end of Remy's neck line. Only the tips of my index finger and thumb seemed to fit safely into the cramped space. "I can't get any leverage." I was reluctant to use much pressure for fear it would tug at the stitches and reopen the wound. "I can't—" It was like trying to open a new jar of jam with tweezers. "It's not—" I started to itch. Just knowing I couldn't use my sterile hands to scratch made me feel as if I were suddenly infested with lice. "It's stuck!" I cried out, rubbing my tormented ears against the tip of my shoulder.

The nurse moved in with her ox-taming hands. "There, I've loosened it for you. Now proceed."

Graham was enrapt. His mother was performing an intricate, specialized task, and it occurred to me that some permanent impression of women in clutch situations would be formed in these next few minutes. I pulled off the cap and reached for the first syringe.

"No!" A firm hand interceded. "All the exterior joints have to be cleaned first. You've got an exposed entry now."

"What? What do you mean, exposed entry?" She quickly pinched off the end of the cap with a Betadine wipe. "The way I learned, there was never an exposed entry—there was an intermediate layer. It had a little rubber thingy on the end!"

The nurse cut me off with a forceful grunt. "Take the line back and continue wiping it with Betadine."

I could sense Graham wide-eyed and assessing. I flashed on all the articles I'd read that insisted moms should change the oil and cut the occasional plank so their sons could see they were fit for the tasks. But I had no desire to change car oil and I would no more trust myself to operate a circular saw than I would the baby nail clippers. I retrieved the line and started wiping.

"Do you recall seeing a small red cap in your supply kit?" the nurse asked.

"There're about ten thousand caps in there."

"I'm asking about a red one—there would only be a handful of them."

"Yeah, I think I saw some. Yes. In the smaller box."

"Keep wiping for one minute," she added as she left the room.

"The hospital said thirty seconds."

"I prefer sixty. Make those nice firm strokes—it's the friction that rids the surface of germs."

I rubbed firmly back and forth and muttered in my own defense, "What Mommy's doing is very, very tricky, honey.

149

I worked really hard to learn it and now it's all different."

"I know, Mom. I know," Graham said.

"It's kind of like if you spent all week working on the letter *G* and then you come in one day and they say there's going to be a really big test on the letter *Q*. It's not that you're not capable of doing the letter *Q*, it's just not what you practiced for."

"All right," she said, rejoining me with a red cap in hand. "This usually goes on the bottles, but it's compatible with the syringes and I think it will make the entrance point feel more similar to what you are used to. That's enough Betadine," she said, adapting the makeshift cap. "You don't want it to puddle."

I survived the next three steps unscathed. The syringe was now screwed in tight and ready to flush. "Open the neck clamp—then press down." I could feel the salty fluid yielding to the weight of my thumb and flooding directly into my daughter's veins.

"Good. Now, continuing to hold the base of the neck line still with your left hand, uncap the tip of the acyclovir bag," the nurse said. Two-handed tasks would now have to be done one-handed.

"Okay," I responded, gathering steam. "The acyclovir tip is open."

"All right. Now, holding the acyclovir tip very still in your right hand, go ahead and loosen the syringe."

I looked at my two fully occupied hands. "With what?"

"Just free up a few fingers."

"They don't come individually—they're part of a hand. I've got the neck line in my left one and the tip of the bag in my right." It felt like I was knee deep in a game of Twister and someone threw a Rubik's Cube between my legs and said with a sinister grin, *Now let's see what you're really made of.* "It would be a miracle if I could undo the syringe at all, let alone without either of these exposed entries bumping into anything."

"Just transfer the acyclovir tip to your ring and baby fingers," she said, which, roughly translated, meant, *Don't look at me like it's impossible because this is how it's done.* "Once you get the acyclovir tip down to those end fingers, your index finger and thumb will be free to unscrew the syringe."

I burrowed my nose in my armpit, brushing it back and forth frantically for relief. "You want me to move this acyclovir tip down between my ring and baby fingers? I have no idea how I'll even accomplish that, but let's just say that I do—without touching anything, of course—"

"Please stop wasting time. I don't want these lines open too long."

"It's impossible!"

"It's not impossible."

"Maybe not for a nurse. Maybe not for a fucking cyborg!"

"Heath, please—" Lon said.

"What? I don't care. It's impossible."

I thought about the alternatives. There were none. Remy couldn't go back to the hospital. This nurse was not going to come to my house every eight hours for the next twenty-one days. Lon wouldn't have been able to get up to speed any faster than I did and I was already three days ahead of him. From the look on his face, I could see he was relieved the job was not his.

"You're doing great, really," Lon said gently.

"Yeah, Mom, really—you can do it," Graham added.

"I hate this," I grumbled, fingers at the ready. As it turned out, getting the acyclovir tip between my ring and baby fingers was not the hard part; repositioning it between my thumb and forefinger was. *Shit!* My hand started to cramp. *Fuck!* My fingers spasmed, then collapsed. *Goddamn it!* And down it went, the virgin tip, cascading off Remy's frowzy pj's and onto Lon's three-day-old jeans. "I told you I couldn't do this!" I shouted, then fled the room.

When the nurse approached me moments later, it was as if nothing had ever happened. "Now, do you feel able to administer the two A.M. dose yourself or would you like me to come back?" Had that question been asked by anyone else, I would have burst out laughing. But the nurse sat stone-faced as ever, and I realized she expected an answer.

"Does it seem to you like I'm in any way ready to do this alone?"

"I think once you calm down you'll be fine."

"How am I supposed to calm down? Every time I move a muscle someone screams about the possibility of infection."

It was this that was killing me. I knew there must be some margin for error but I couldn't figure out what it was—it kept moving. In my work, if I got a little careless, I might scar the page with an uninspired adjective. But no one ever died from my mistakes.

"If you need me at two, I will be here at two," she said. "That's my job. But at two, I will expect you to do this yourself. I will only be here to supervise. Your daughter's care is now up to you. Whether you put it off one time or two, it doesn't really matter. Sooner or later, you're going to have to start doing this."

The alarm went off at 1:30 A.M. I bolted up and headed to the kitchen—adrenaline pumping, bowels stirring, jittery with the late night chill. Shortly after the nurse had left, I'd chugged a beer and gotten out my yellow pad, visualizing each step in my mind, translating what I knew from the old props to the new ones, making the connections, repeating the tasks out loud and coming up with a detailed breakdown of each and every movement, including choreographed reminders of where each finger needed to be when. *Step one: Take acyclovir out of the fridge, bring to room temperature. . . .* I used this time to make my preparations, working by flashlight like a cat burglar. By two o'clock, I was ready to begin.

I fanned out the loaded syringes, the wipes, the tape and the hand grenade in a circular pattern around Remy's head as she slept. I flushed her line. I moved all the right fingers in all the right places. I screwed the acyclovir pouch in place and waited till I could sense the subtle contractions inside the bag as the medicine began to flow out. *Tick, tick, tick.* I lay on the living-room couch while the fluid ran . . . *tick, tick, tick* . . . my rest syncopated by a kitchen timer set to go off in fifty-five minutes. *Buzz.* I flew to the crib. The sack was drained. I was nearly home free. I loosened the acyclovir tip, my fingers growing more facile with each gesture. I injected the saline, flushing the line clean. Just two more steps: Flush with heparin and recap with a new blue plug, and I could add "administering intravenous medications" to my resumé and go back to sleep.

To eliminate unnecessary exposures, the nurse had suggested I leave the final syringe of heparin screwed into the bottleneck—sticking straight up—until I needed it. That is where it was at 4:07 A.M., in the dark room, lit only by a flashlight bulb that was shining on Remy's neck and not on the ironing board butted up under the lip of the crib's end. I reached over, groping for the bottle until— *ohhh, nooooo*—my hand whacked up against the syringe and sent the whole thing toppling to the floor, bouncing on the unvacuumed rug as if in slow motion.

By the time I'd rescrubbed, reprepped, completed the flush, inspected the crib for chokeable debris and tiptoed back to bed, it was nearly five o'clock. Remy awakened for a feeding shortly thereafter. Her phenobarbital was due at eight. There would be breakfast, a nursing, another acyclovir, then lunch. An increasingly runny nose needed constant wiping, and a diaper rash brought on by the diarrhea from the medication needed special creams and a watchful eye—we couldn't risk a secondary source of infection. There were more nursings throughout the afternoon, then dinner, her next IV, her evening pheno, her bedtime nursing, a nightmare that could not be soothed by Lon, but only by my milky breasts. If I was lucky, there would be an hour of sleep before the alarm called me back to the crib, to my list and my vials and obstacles in the dark.

Through this humbling process of mind-numbing detail and inexorable exhaustion, I lost all perspective, and soon all hope. Twenty-four hours after returning home, I became convinced that the reason I had felt so many angels around my daughter was that they were getting ready to take her.

12.

teach your children well

For a man whose ashes were dissolved at sea at fifty-three, my dad was full of words to live by.

"Any man who doesn't believe in life insurance, let him die once without it," he would say, paraphrasing Will Rogers and boosting his own sizable earnings as an expert salesman. By the age of thirty, he was the number-one life insurance salesman in the country; a "self-made man" was the term I often heard, distinguishing him from the old-money friends he sought to keep up with.

"If the queen had balls, she'd be king," was another one of his favorites—questionable in couth, but startlingly feminist and clearly indicative of the high hopes he had for his daughter.

"I'd rather have a bottle in front of me than a frontal lobotomy." That was the charades clue my dad handed me one time to act out for a group of his friends. I had no idea what it meant—I was eight—but I could break anything down into syllables. Four minutes later, there was a good deal of talk about us going to Las Vegas for some big father-daughter charades tournament (can you imagine anything more exciting in the whole wide world?), but I never heard another word about it after that night.

"Your father would like to talk to you. He says it's important," said the peeved flight attendant who'd been ordered to fetch me from coach for a meeting with my dad up in first class. Although we were on the same trip, our seats were, inexplicably, not together. Even at fourteen, I was more relieved than disappointed. I pulled back the blue curtain to find my dad wrestling with the last drops of his Bloody Mary—*tap, tap*—the ice avalanching down his chin and into his lap.

"Oh, good. There you are. I've been making a list for you," he said. "There are things you need to read. Things you need to understand."

"All right, Dad."

I waited for him to give me the list, but he did not. He continued in hushed tones, and I wondered if we were being followed or bugged or if he had some reason to think we wouldn't get a chance to talk again.

"The key to life," he said, summoning great expectations,

157

"is in the book *Atlas Shrugged*. Have you heard of it?"

"Yes," I replied. He had been telling me about it for as long as I could remember.

"It's by Ayn Rand."

"Yes, I know."

"People like you and me need our own set of rules. Promise me you'll read it."

"I promise."

"Everything you need to know about life is in that book. All right," he said, and then added the most shocking, unexpected thing of all: "You can go back now." I returned in a daze, pressing my forehead against the lukewarm plastic window and vowing never — not for a very long time, if ever — to read that book.

My father had often told me the story of some great ancestor of ours named Rufus Choate. He had been a prominent attorney during the late 1800s in Boston and was famous for his courtroom theatrics. The most famous tale was of the time when, finding himself increasingly annoyed with the judge, he got up, approached the bench and, with a broad cavalier sweep, turned to face the gallery, arms firmly crossed. "Mr. Choate," the judge bellowed, "are you trying to show your contempt for this court?" To which my ancestor replied, "No, Your Honor, I'm trying to conceal it."

There was a painting of Rufus Choate hanging in Boston's revered Faneuil Hall. Or so I'd been told. I had walked past that building every single day en route from my little North End boardinghouse room to my cubicle in a Back Bay high-rise, but I had never gone inside — didn't want to know—until the day I got word that my father had gone into his third coma in so many years and I decided it was time to call his bluff. I wanted proof so I could write him off once and for all.

I stormed the red-carpeted stairs of Faneuil Hall, suitcase in hand. My eyes traveled across the high-domed wall of portraits until ... *behind you.* I spun around and came face-to-face with an oil painting the size of a lap pool. It was like looking in a mirror. This man, this Rufus Choate, could have been my twin brother. A docent approached excitedly. "Let me tell you a story about this man ... ," he said. I knew it by heart, every word, every gavel, every gesture.

Great. *Just great.* The one thing that turns out to be true and it's that I come from a long line of arrogant pricks.

The summer after Remy was born I read a study in the newspaper. It said that nine out of ten white teenage girls disliked their bodies. For black teenage girls, it was only one in four. The white girls defined the ideal in terms of Barbie-esque measurements, where the black girls defined it as the right attitude. Of their mothers, the best thing the white teens could say was that it was possible they had once been attractive in their youth. The predominant black teen response was that they saw their mothers as strong, powerful role models.

This did not surprise me.

Whatever black mothers got from whatever they believed had always seemed to me, an outsider, to be pure and sentient and unpoliticized: It helped them to cope, to endure, to nurture, to heal, to reach out and to love, and, despite all odds, to raise strong, respectful children who admired their mothers.

And so it was in my early years of motherhood that I started gobbling up the words of Marian Wright Edelman and Maya Angelou, who brought poetry to the masses and urged us all to say, "simply, quite simply, Good Morning." And I began tuning in to the white woman's favorite black friend, Oprah Winfrey, as she slowly and systematically began to engage millions of viewers each day in a dialogue about spirituality and God: There were chats with Deepak Chopra and Marianne Williamson. There were panels with the writers of *The Celestine Prophecy* and *The Road Less Traveled*. There were rabbis and reverends, atheists and the ACLU.

One day when Remy was a few months old, we lay across my bed nursing and watching Oprah with the volume down low. There was a couple on from North Carolina. They were white, almost corpselike, and they spoke in great detail about the responsibility they had for beating their children. *Look at their faces,* I shouted in silence. *Where is the light?* There were video clips from their home life in which they showed off their assortment of discipline sticks, including a nice fat portable one they kept in the glove compartment for any shenanigans that might occur on the road. *That's not discipline, that's hate*. I scooted closer to the TV, clutching Remy like a football spot-welded to my nipple. "C'mon, stand up!" I shouted. "Somebody say it." I sat inches from the screen, ears pricked like a Labrador's, and waited to hear the truth. *These people are evil.*

Some audience members disapproved of their methods, while others went on to debate the merits of spanking. The wan, mouse-eyed couple from the South held their ground, justifying their position with the phrase "spare the rod, spoil the child," while viewing clips of their young daughters being whacked across the backside. Oprah, it seemed, trusted her viewers to see things for what they were; she held her tongue loudly, and in doing so, handed her smack-happy guests a nice long rope.

About other things, Oprah was less reserved. I don't know if it was my predisposition to hear it or Oprah's increased need to preach it, but during my pregnancy with Remy, and in her first months of life, it seemed that hardly a week went by when Oprah didn't turn to her audience and say, "Why are you here, people? This is the question each and every one of us needs to ask ourselves." And on this she pressed down hard: "What have you been put on this planet to do?"

There was something else that Oprah referred to quite often. It was her understanding of how God got in touch with those of us who weren't listening. "First," Oprah said, "He kicks a little sand your way. Then a pebble. Then a rock. Then He sets up a little bitty wall and crashes you right into it. If that doesn't work, He erects a bigger wall. And a bigger one, and on and on, until you get it."

It never occurred to me that she meant it literally.

It was midafternoon and the traffic on the 405 was moving at a fast clip. I wasn't late for the baby-sitter, but it occurred to me that I could be. I went with the flow of traffic, which was close to seventy. I was restless and impatient. I pushed one radio button, then another; nothing was agreeable. "Fucking commercials!" I pushed a tape into the stereo and whipped my head over my left shoulder to check for cars in the fast lane. All clear. I tilted left—*shit!* I pulled the wheel hard to the right, away from the large white object that had suddenly appeared in the left lane. My van swerved out of control and into the lane on my right. *Shit, oh god, oh no.* I pulled it back, harder, tighter, overcompensating so much that it spun completely around and propelled me back across the middle lane, the fast lane and straight toward the center divider. *Oh god, oh god, I'm going to die, please, no . . . God.* The van hit so hard it bounced off the wall and spun back around another ninety degrees, ultimately coming to rest in the lane I had started in, facing the oncoming traffic dead on.

The man in the car behind me, whose face I was now looking straight into, offered a reassuring smile and indicated that he was getting help with his car phone. A sunny blond woman my mother's age appeared at the passenger door and got inside. She had been driving the white car I had failed to see. "Do you have a baby back there?" she said, scanning the back of the van.

"I'm so sorry. I'm so sorry. I didn't see you . . ."

"Shhh, shhh," she said, gently patting my hand. "It's okay, sweetie, everything's going to be all right."

Seconds later—literally, seconds—a tan, outdoorsy fellow with a mustache came up to me at the window. "Hi, how are you? I'm a paramedic. How many fingers am I holding up?"

"You're a paramedic?"

"How many fingers?"

"Three."

He continued to observe me as he spoke. "I was just on my way home from the beach when I saw it happen—I was in the lane next to you." Despite the fact that the traffic had been moving at nearly seventy miles per hour and that I had careened multiple times across three lanes, no other car was touched.

"Oh god, oh god, everything's getting all tingly and black, it's all pins and needles. . . . I'm so scared."

"Okay, hold my hand and breathe," said the paramedic.

"I can't see, I can't see. My eyes are open, but I can't see." It was like being blacked out and conscious at the same time.

"We're right here with you, sweetie," lulled the beachy grandmother, who had settled into the passenger seat and had no apparent plans to move on.

"Do you feel like you're going to faint?" the paramedic continued.

"No, not really—it's just all pins and needles and dark."

"Can you move your neck?"

I tried. "It hurts."

"Okay, let's just leave it still."

"I can wiggle my toes. Doesn't that mean it's not broken?"

"Let's just wait till the ambulance gets here, all right?"

My vision started to clear. I saw one police car, then another. There were five on the scene by the time the ambulance came. *This must be really serious. I'm in a serious car accident. Oh my god, what if my neck is broken? Is this how it happens? Just like that?* My friend the paramedic moved out of earshot to update the police. It was decided I would be moved on a board. I sat very still as they collared my neck, then slid the board behind me. I was flipped sideways and strapped down and carried out of my car.

"You need anything from in here? Your purse or anything?" asked one of the ambulance drivers.

"Yeah, my purse," I said to the sky, while blue and red lights flickered in the periphery.

"Anything else?"

"I don't know. What else do I need?"

"Well, the van will be impounded. It may be a while before you get it back."

"Oh. Well, there's a bag of sand toys in the back. If you could just grab that, okay?"

My worldly possessions were piled on top of my feet and I was lifted up into the ambulance. We crawled through the traffic jam that had been created by me and by the onlookers trying to see what happened to me and headed off to the ER.

My neck was not broken, although it would be hours before I knew that for sure. I just kept wiggling my toes and my fingers and trying to get some medical passerby to verify that this meant that all was well, but no one would. To the medical world, I was a nonemergency. The fact that a brush with death had triggered in me a psychic upheaval of seismic proportions was, I suppose, not really their department.

It was then I began to think of angels, which was hardly a dangerous leap of faith; angels were the pop icon of the decade. There were angel cards and angel posters, angel pins and angel lunch boxes. *There are angels watching over me,* I realized that night as I lay in bed trying to breathe through the threatening stiffness. I lay flat on my back with my legs slightly spread and my arms loosely out at my sides and I allowed the accident to play over and over in my mind, not tensing, not resisting, but letting it play itself out. *There are angels watching over me.* I was told that the pain and stiffness would be much worse the second day, but they were not. I continued to let the accident run through me and to think of angels and to recognize this comforting truth: *Someone wants me alive. Someone wants me here. I have important work to do on this planet.*

As the days passed and the pain lessened and the story was told and retold, I would refer always to the angels—"Oh yes, well, I am very, very lucky—there are obviously angels watching over me"—but they became somehow in the telling less celestial and more cherubic, like imps or fairies or the Keebler elves. In time, I managed to whittle the whole experience down to the one aspect I found most appealing: In the grand scheme of things, I must be very important.

13.

the truth is out there

When we first got home from UCLA, I was hanging on by a nail—a hangnail, even. Slowly, one IV at a time, I had strengthened my grip, clambered my way back up, and was now, on our fifth day home, standing upright.

I plopped Remy in a Sassy seat, distracted her with Cheerios and, slipping in from behind, manipulated my caps and syringes to complete the thirty-two steps for her morning acyclovir. "Graham, honey, teeth—we're leaving in five minutes." I was not exactly sashaying across the tightrope that had become my life, but I was nonetheless balancing. Lon took Remy into the other room to ply her with pheno-

167

barbital. I sat at the kitchen table, drinking coffee and reading the paper, unfazed by her screams of protest or Lon's syrupy crimson shirt upon their return. "And don't forget to wear underpants—you're going to the doctor's right after school," I shouted to Graham from across the house. His fifth birthday was the next day, and I was preparing to turn somersaults. We had invited four friends to descend upon the yard in costume, bash open a piñata, and pick the plastic characters off the top of an overpriced superhero theme cake. I figured I could weave these activities in between Remy's afternoon IV, a breastfeeding, and nap time. I had it planned out in fifteen-minute increments. I had it all written down on a yellow pad.

At 11:00 A.M., Remy started to run a temperature—the first in ten days, the first since she had the arterial line inserted in her jugular. By the time we got to Dr. Vasquez's office for Graham's noon appointment, Remy's fever had spiked to 102.4°. Lon took her into one examining room while I sat with my son, waiflike in his X-Men underpants, in another. The nurse took him through an eye exam. He missed almost every symbol, although I knew his eyesight was perfect. This was to have been his big day; his big-boy checkup at our new doctor's. But Remy's wails were incessant and distance did nothing to mute them. I headed for the door.

"No! Don't leave me," Graham begged, starting to cry.

"Real quick, baby. I'll be right back. I just need to check." I ran out into the hall and saw Dr. Vasquez placing a call at the nurses' station. "Well," she said to me, cupping the receiver, "she has a double ear infection. That could easily account for the pain and the fever, but with the catheter in I'm not going to take anything for granted. Her neck seems floppy to me—she could be getting septic—" She stopped, returning to the receiver. "Dr. Deville, this is Dr. Vasquez. I'm calling about Remy Davis. . . ." My ears went numb as she spoke to the doctors at UCLA and I gripped my shivering son, who had run out in the hall to be with me. Dr. Vasquez hung up the phone.

"Can we all be together while you do his exam?" I asked.

"Sure," she said as we moved into the room where Remy was. "So listen, I'm going to treat the ear infection with amoxicillin, but we're going to need to get a blood sample—you'll have to take her over to the lab this afternoon, okay? The nurse will give you an authorization form," she said, then took a breath and switched charts. "So, now, this is Graham, right? Well, buddy, I'm sorry about all this. You holding up okay?"

"Yeah," he said in a wisp of voice.

"So, five years old. Big boy now, huh? Here, come stand here and face the wall—we'll take a look. Do you know when your birthday is?" He stood as straight as a toy soldier as she checked his bone structure, running her hand down his spine, asking him to bend at the hip.

"Yeah. October twenty-third."

"Oh . . ." It seemed that she stopped listening for a moment, her hands on his narrow hips.

"My birthday party is tomorrow."

"Yeah?" she said, and turned to Lon and me. Remy was

169

now asleep in his arms. "One leg appears to be longer than the other."

"Is that unusual?" I asked.

"Well, it's about half an inch off—that's quite a bit." She turned to Graham. "Does your hip ever hurt when you're playing?"

I stared at him, waiting. "No," he said.

"No," I added. "He's never said anything about that."

"Well, that's good. Okay, pal, let's hop up on the table." She continued her exam as images of Forrest Gump flashed in front of me. Dr. Vasquez pressed a stethoscope against his chest and called my attention back to the exam. "Have you ever been told he has a heart murmur?" It was almost vaudevillian.

"What? No, he's never had anything. He's always been perfectly healthy."

"Well, he's got one now. Does he seem to have trouble keeping up with the other kids at school?"

"No," I said, the room growing tight, "he's really active. I mean, you know, after he's been jumping on the bed he sometimes says he's tired and sits down, but then he jumps back up ten seconds later." Remy woke with a start. I reached out to hold her, struggling to keep a passive face. "Okay, baby, Mama's here."

"Do his lips ever turn blue?" the doctor asked matter-of-factly.

"No—not that I—"

"No," Lon added.

"Well, it's probably just a benign murmur, but it is one of the more pronounced ones I've heard. Here, take a listen." Lon rose and placed the stethoscope to his ears.

"Can we discuss this some other time? I mean, I really just can't deal with this right now, okay? He's fine. I know he's fine. He's the healthiest kid I know." It was then I remembered the poem by Kahlil Gibran.

Your children are not your children.
They are the sons and daughters of Life's longing for itself.
They come through you but not from you,
And though they are with you, yet they belong not to you. . . .

I had heard the poem for the first time at the funeral of my cousin's fiancé. He was a handsome, winning UCLA grad cum law student when he got hit by a car while crossing the street. Graham was a toddler at the time and I could remember thinking, *What's the point?* A mother spends a lifetime reminding her children to look both ways before crossing. She worries for years about the fatal dangers of city streets, until finally, her kids go off to college and she feels safe in transitioning to subtler fears, like careers and mates and what one believes in. As we stood atop the hills of Forest Lawn, hundreds of fresh-scrubbed young faces blotchy with tears and disillusionment, that poem was read. I looked at the dead boy's mother, so still, so composed, and could see that she understood it, had probably even selected it; that even in her grief she realized that our children are not ours to keep; that the arc of their lives may not sway or extend or ultimately break according to any chronology we can envision. It frightened me to recognize that. To get it. *Does that mean I'm the kind of person who could cope with losing a child?*

As I sat in the doctor's office that day rocking my feverish daughter with the arterial catheter and the brain lesion, my grasp on reality was slipping like wet silt on a fire-ravaged hill. I clung by my fingertips and descended into even murkier water. *Who was that basketball player? Gathers. Hank Gathers. Didn't he have a heart murmur? Had his mom sat on the bench every day of his life watching for his lips to turn blue?* I didn't have to wonder if she was there when he dropped dead; I had seen her on the news.

"Listen," I heard Dr. Vasquez say, "I know you're overwhelmed right now, but this *is* Graham's appointment, and that *is* why he's here—so I can examine him."

"I know, I'm sorry, I just . . ."

"I'm going to consult with the other doctors here in the group, see what they say. I may want Graham to be seen over at UCLA." I thought immediately of David, of his daughter's malformed heart, and whether or not it was still beating. "They have an outstanding pediatric cardiology department—we may want to have him tested over there."

I reached for something—a chair—but was already sitting. *God doesn't give you more than you can handle.* The words brushed past me like comfort offered by some bosomy grandmother pulling me in and calling me "child." But the words brought no comfort. If God doesn't give you more than you can handle, I knew we were in big trouble.

Lon took Remy to the lab for a blood draw and I took Graham for ice cream. I watched his lips. I watched him run from the car to the house. I placed my hand on his chest, nonchalantly, and counted. *What if this whole Remy thing has been just a warm-up for the real Big Dive—Graham's Big Dive? Will he become the little boy who has to sit on the sidelines? What will he look like with a foot-long scar on his chest?* But real and present danger superseded the merely possible.

The first phone call was at 7:00 P.M. "Remy's white count is very high," said the serious young doctor who was on call when the test results were rushed back from the lab. "According to her chart, it's higher than anything she's had so far. I'm going to consult with her team at UCLA now. You might want to make preparations to go back to the hospital tonight."

I dropped the phone. My tongue was numb and dry. Graham could see he was losing me. "Time for books, remember?" he said in earnest.

"Not right now," I said, pushing past him to get to Lon. "We might have to go back to UCLA tonight. They said her white count is high."

"It's probably just the cold," Lon said, not taking his eyes off Remy. "I don't want you going back."

"You said right after they called. You promised," Graham said, books in hand.

"I know I did, but now I've got to get organized. Mommy and Rem might have to go back to the hospital for a while."

"But you haven't even read me a book for ... forty-hundred days."

"I don't know what's going on right now. I'm very worried. I can't deal with reading to you right now, okay?" *Don't yell at the poor thing, he has a bad heart.*

"Okay."

"I'm sorry, baby. I just can't do it."

"It's okay," he said, and I realized then how many times in the past few weeks he had had to say just that.

"I'm sorry," I repeated, wishing I were the kind of person who could just sit calmly and read with him until we knew more. Instead, I sat by the phone making notes ... *pick up cake, string piñata, recharge camera battery.* I had my list. I could turn it over to my mom and our neighbors, and Graham could still have his birthday party. My bags were packed, and people who knew about these things would be checking on Remy shortly. The phone rang again around eight o'clock.

"Well, I've spoken to Dr. Deville over at UCLA and he doesn't think you need to come in tonight."

"What? Why not?" I asked, thrown.

"He feels he'd rather just have you watch her there for the night."

"Watch her for what?"

"Fussiness, listlessness, irritability—Dr. Deville feels

174

from his meetings with you at the hospital that you're more than capable of assessing her condition and acting appropriately."

"I don't want to act appropriately. Her white count is up. You guys are obviously concerned. Now *I'm* the one who's supposed to decide if it's serious? I don't want to decide. You're the doctors. Why don't you decide?"

"Listen, Mrs. Davis. At this point we really won't know what's going on until things go one way or the other. So why don't you just try to relax and get some sleep . . ."

"How the fuck am I supposed to be in charge of assessing her situation if I'm asleep?"

"If something's really wrong, she'll wake up. You have a monitor in her room, right?"

"Yeah. It was there the night she started seizing, too."

"Well, she's on anticonvulsants now, so that shouldn't be a problem."

For a moment neither of us spoke. "I just . . . ," I started, then stopped.

"We'll know more in the morning, okay?"

I began again, still unsure of where a full sentence might lead. "It's just . . ."

"If you need anything, please—"

"I just feel . . ." The noise in my head was like a vacuum; I couldn't form a single thought.

"Mrs. Davis, I really need to go now."

Then I knew what it was. "I just feel so alone."

"You shouldn't feel that way. I'm right here."

"Right where? You're not here to feel her face. You're not

here to look at the neck site and decide if the red is normal red or inflamed red. You've never even met her." I stopped, wondering if she ever would.

"All I can say is, we'll know more in the morning. Until then, just do your best to sleep, and if you need anything, please call me."

I hung up the phone and dropped my head to my hands, a frail silhouette against a menacing sky. *I am alone.* Graham was next door playing with a neighbor. *I am totally alone.* Lon was rocking Remy to sleep. *I am utterly and completely alone.* The quiet was like a tornado sweeping past me. *And I am so very tired.* The words knocked me out flat and I stayed there gladly. *Take me, please, just take me.* I opened my hands, letting them lie malleable and unresisting in my lap, and I succumbed to the maelstrom. *You win.* It was a numb, mindless free fall, torrential yet still. For several moments, I did not move a muscle, not even to breathe.

And then I rose, clearing a dish, collecting stray socks, drifting through the tasks at hand, utterly and completely void. Nothing occurred to me. I was no longer there.

Lon emerged from Remy's room. "All quiet."

"Mm," I said almost imperceptibly. I did not ask if Remy felt warm; if she fussed when he rocked her; if the skin around the catheter entrance looked all right. I did not ask a thing. He held me tight, but I did not dissolve.

"You okay?"

"Mm-hmm."

"Sure?"

"Mm-hmm," I sounded, pulling back, moving robotically

through the house, gathering stray Tinkertoys, checking my IV supplies, wiping down the rectal thermometer.

"I'm going to go get Graham, get him in bed," Lon announced softly as he headed for the door. "*X-Files* is on in ten minutes."

This was our special end-of-the-week ritual; we hadn't missed an episode since its premiere. The opening credits blazed past me with their haunting, conspiratorial music, and I disappeared effortlessly into the episode. I felt no urge to check on Remy. I felt no irresistible train of thought careening off into morbid possibilities. The duality of voices—*she's going to die / oh no she's not*—had ceased to exist. It was almost like any other Friday of the year. Almost, but not quite. The show was halfway over before I finally noticed why. There was a feeling, leaning quietly, like a stranger in the doorway. A feeling so unlikely, I had to sit up just to identify it.

Happiness? No. It smiled like happiness but it didn't skip and wriggle and fly off in giddy loop-de-loops. *Contentment?* Not exactly. It was more glowing, less flat. *Peace? Hmm* . . . I was not as familiar with that one. *Peace,* as in calm. *Peace,* as in the soothing quiet in my brain. *Peace,* as in the absence of fear or anxiety.

So this is peace.

I was no longer alone or afraid or concerned. *Everything is going to be fine.* I laid my head back down, this time in Lon's lap, like a newlywed. *Remy is going to be fine.* He rubbed my neck, and I clasped his hand, feeling the edge of his gold band pressing against my fingers. *You are not alone.* It was in the gentle squeeze of this hand that I had been both thrilled and comforted for going on a decade. It was under the touch of this hand that my son and daughter were conceived and with the reassurance of this hand that I cared for them. It was in the warmth of this hand, both soft and strong, that I had been shown the meaning of love in human terms, and it was in the company of this hand that I was intended to grow. *What God hath brought together.* He brushed his fingertips along my palm, my wrist, and we ate a bowl of ice cream with one spoon. I started Remy's ten o'clock IV. She slept peacefully and without fever throughout the night.

When I finished her 6:00 A.M. meds Remy was bright-eyed and bushy-tailed, with reassuring green gunk oozing from her nose. Everyone felt comfortable attributing the high white count and fever to a cold and an ear infection, and life resumed, but not like before. After that night when quiet despair was caressed and exalted—that night of pure, unmistakable grace—I no longer walked on the wire; I was carried, my feet brushing the surfaces of the day like a whisper and gliding steadily above the fray.

On Sunday morning I went to church alone. Shortly after Pastor Ken had greeted the congregation he invited us to reach out to a neighbor, to exchange the peace of the Lord. *Peace of the Lord? Peace. Oh my gosh . . .* I had never understood what it meant, so I had never said it, always turning and offering a safe, friendly "Good morning."

A plump, gray-haired woman who attended each Sunday

with her large, close-knit family tapped me on the shoulder. "Peace of the Lord," she said.

"Yes. Peace of the Lord," I echoed.

She stopped, and with a gentle double take looked deeply into my watery eyes. "You got it, didn't you?"

Her intuition was stunning. "Yes."

We sat down. I looked up at the cross, wondering if it would strike me differently somehow. I listened to the Bible reading, thinking that possibly the seas would part and the text would now reverberate with great clarity, but I still found the words cumbersome and foreign.

The big-kids' choir was scheduled to sing, and on that day they sang in pure, poignant, two-part harmony, "Shepherd me, O God, beyond my wants, beyond my fears, from death into life." I did not know that the lyrics were taken from the Twenty-third Psalm. I just knew that they were the most beautiful and relevant words I had ever heard. *Is that what this is all about? This gift of peace, this calm, this freedom from fear—freedom from fearing death, Remy's death, my death, Graham's death, Lon's death. Any death. Not because they will not occur, but because they need not be feared.* My life had become overrun with fear. But now it had been lifted from me and I felt a greater sense of peace than I had ever known. *This is God. This is His presence.* It had nothing to do with rules. It was not based on memorizing Bible passages or denying the rights of this group or that. It had no petitions to sign or pleasures to revoke. It had no conditions. It knew me well, all the parts of me. Every flaw, every hurt, every conflict, every good intention. It was not a group activity. It was a gift from God to me, to free me, to make my life joyously livable, untrammeled by the mortal snags and chains—the petty thoughts, the resentments, the corrosive anger—and to reconcile my beleaguered soul. I had never felt anything so deeply, or with such certainty, in my entire life.

Later that week I would find myself sitting in a Lutheran orientation class required for new school parents. Pastor Ken gave us each a handout with the Bible passage "Thou shalt worship no other gods but me." I had heard it before, taking it as further proof of the provincial, closed-minded, chauvinistic views of the Christian church.

"Mammon, or money," Ken said, "is usually the other god they're referring to." *Oh.* I stood corrected as my thoughts began to shift like sand in a timer. *Was this whole money thing an issue even back then?* "One can either worship Mammon or God, but one cannot worship both," Ken said, expounding. *Is that true?* I knew I didn't worship Mammon. In fact, I'd spent the better part of the past decade running from Mammon's clutches because deep in the heart of wherever these certainties lie, I knew that the pursuit of it led nowhere I wanted to be. I wasn't clear on where exactly that was, only that it was related somehow to love and accountability and a meaningful use of one's gifts. But now here I was, being blindsided with the news that what I thought was my own personal and hard-won philosophy was in fact one of the key tenets of a two-thousand-year-old religion. And not just any religion, but one that I'd come to view with smug disdain based (there was no getting around it now) purely on circumstantial evidence. It had to be. I had no firsthand knowledge of whatever the Bible did or didn't say. It was right about the Mammon thing, I knew that. Maybe, I thought, just maybe, it had some light to shed on other weighty issues, too.

There was no turning back. In one ironic glimmer, it now seemed possible that all the wisdom I'd ever craved might be right there in that old book. And had been all along.

The truth is funny that way.

14.

signing off

In an ideal world we would have been able to eliminate the need for Remy's thrice-daily IVs on Monday, a week after our return home. But in real life, futuristic machines went on the fritz and reactor strips were nowhere to be found, and ultimately it was Friday before they would make a definitive diagnosis: Remy did not have—nor had she ever had—the herpes virus, in encephalitic form or otherwise. She had a growth in her brain that needed to be taken out surgically. The treatment was stopped and the arterial line was removed from her neck, a process one would like to think of as a slow, gentle coaxing—along the lines of a splinter extraction, say—but in fact is handled more like the tug of a lawn-mower cord.

It was now time for our appointment with Dr. Warwick Peacock.

In my mind, this was where all the truly horrible information would come, and I had been bracing myself for it since the day we left UCLA. I had imagined a huge, wood-paneled office with a great mahogany desk commensurate in size and authority with the expertise required to perform such a surgery. There would be a sprawling view of the campus behind us. Sparkling water would be offered, but we would decline. We would sit up on the edge of the visitors' chairs like children in the principal's office, and we would start to hear the numbers.

I was convinced that all this casual, euphemistic talk about "good outcomes" and "just fine" and "perfectly normal" would have to come to an end. This would be it. This was where we would get down to brass tacks. I pictured some sort of computer printout with a breakdown of all the statistical probabilities for all the possible atrocities that might be committed in my daughter's brain: *Defective hopscotch potential: 37 percent. Thwarted verbal development: 51 percent. Frequent cutlery dropping: 29 percent. Paralysis and death . . .*

Paralysis and death. I had said those words over and over again to diffuse their potential impact in The Big Meeting. The meeting with the paperwork where we would hear all the terrible truths and then be asked to sign off on them.

Lon and I were getting well acclimated to the various buildings at UCLA. We entered Medical Plaza 200 and

183

found Neurosurgery in the basement. (Had I been thinking clearly, I would have realized then there would be no room with a view.) My eyes were drawn to a flyer for a Brain Tumor Support Group. *Oh shit!* Were we supposed to be joining a brain tumor support group? *I don't want to be in a brain tumor support group. No, wait a minute. That's not us. That's not Remy. Her little thingy's coming out. That would make her ineligible. This must be for the inoperable people,* I decided.

A slim, effervescent black woman approached. "Mr. and Mrs. Davis?" she lilted, to which we nodded blankly. Her smile was so bright, her demeanor so chatty, I wondered if she was aware of the direness of the occasion. She led us down a corridor, past a series of small exam rooms. "I think we'll put you in here," she said, stopping at the first one that was empty. "Dr. Peacock will be by in just a few minutes."

As we sat in wait in the white, metallic room, it occurred to me that we too were now part of some medical research, that the walls had been wired to see if Lon and I would grow squirrelly or weepy or crack under the pressure in some other quantifiable way. The paranoia was interrupted by a voice in the hall. It was distinctly South African, distinctly his. I gulped at the moments like oxygen. The door flew open and a purple tapestry vest came into view. I panned up, past a jewel-toned bow tie. "Hello," Dr. Peacock said with a broad smile. There was another man following close behind him; Dr. Peacock offered an introduction. "This is ... colleague ... England ..." I was so keyed up, I could process only fragments of his sentences. "... mind if he joins us?"

"Oh, no, good, fine," we said in tandem, leaving me to

wonder if this man had come specifically to observe Remy's case or just happened to be passing through. I could feel myself nodding and smiling, but I did not know to what. Every cell in my brain was braced for the deep breath and the "well . . ." that I knew would be interrupting the small talk at any moment.

"Well . . . ," said Dr. Peacock, "as I told you in our meeting at the hospital, I foresee a very good outcome here. It's really just the location that makes things a bit awkward. It's not my favorite place to work, but I go into that area at least once a week and I feel quite comfortable working there if I have to." He started to draw a schematic on a yellow pad to better explain the procedure. "This is where Remy's lesion is," he said, making a dark blue swirl the size of a really large grape. "And this is the brain stem here," he continued, never actually picking his pen up.

"And you can't touch the brain stem, right?" I asked.

"No, you can't—"

"Or what? Paralysis, right?" I interrupted.

"Yes," he said. "Or worse. But I have never had that happen. And I don't foresee it happening here."

He touched briefly on the risks true of all surgeries: problems with anesthesia, problems with infection, none of them much different from what you hear at the dentist's before a root canal, and always countered with "I have never had that happen, and the likelihood is extremely slim." I found all these cheery generalizations quite unsettling. Where were my numbers? Where was my doom and gloom?

Lon sat up, fascinated by the drawing. "So how do you make sure you stop before you reach the brain stem?"

"Well, the brain is encased in a very thin membrane. That is my guideline. I have to whittle away at the lesion, removing as much of it as possible without disturbing the membrane in any way."

"So we don't want anyone sneezing or anything?" I threw in with a nervous laugh. Dr. Peacock and Lon and the doctor from Britain looked at me oddly and returned to the drawing.

"Where do you enter exactly?" Lon asked, suddenly in his element.

Dr. Peacock demonstrated on the drawing with his pen. I struggled to follow but could not—my comprehension of 3-D space and inversions was painfully scant. I flashed on the time I'd tried to windsurf in Fiji and was so totally incapable of grasping the notion of flipping the sail to catch the wind that I was well on my way to Uluwatu before some hotel umbrella boys were called out to rescue me.

"I don't understand," I said with my face in a scrunch. "Can you just show me on my head, please?"

Dr. Peacock took his hands and placed them on my skull, gently turning it sideways to feature my temple area. He took his pen and pointed directly above the highest point of my ear. "We'll enter somewhere in here, then work our way to the center. We have a very special machine—it's quite high-tech, really, truly amazing—that will measure out all the points in Remy's skull and brain and tell us the optimal entry point for minimizing the loss of gray matter."

"So everything you cut through, you lose?" Lon asked.

"Yes. There is no other way to get to the center. But we are talking about a very slim section here. If we were to take this same amount out of your brain tomorrow," he said, now looking at me, "you'd never know the difference."

"Oh," I said, unsure if this was a slight or a reassurance.

"As far as her speech and language development go"—*oh boy, here it comes*—"I think it's highly unlikely we'll have any problems. The lesion is several centimeters away from where we usually find the speech and language center of the brain in children. And at her age, even if that area was disturbed, the skill would simply be transferred over to the other side. I saw a little girl yesterday—took out her entire speech and language center a few years back. Now you can hardly get a word in."

"So there's just a big gap in her head, then?" Lon asked.

"After the procedure, we fill the void with saline. Over time that will be absorbed and replaced with spinal fluid, which eventually will encourage the two sides to expand somewhat." Lon nodded. I nodded. The doctor from Britain nodded. "So, do you have any questions?" Dr. Peacock said, brows lifted.

"Would you mind signing the drawing?" Lon asked.

"Seriously?" He blushed.

"For the baby book." Lon had developed some mind-boggling ability to view this whole event in the past tense. I watched as Dr. Peacock scrawled his name above the harmless-looking scribbles; I studied his hands. Then I heard words coming from my own mouth. "God has given you beautiful hands to save the babies with."

Dr. Peacock didn't bat an eye. "And that is who deserves all the credit. He is the one that guides me. In fact, if you want to help, that's what you can do. I need your prayers. Lots of them." His tone was utterly devoid of drama, yet they were the most galvanizing words I'd ever heard.

That night I began to pray. Not just moments of passing thought couched in the notion of *Ohgodohgodohgod,* but specifically and with intention. I had no idea what I was doing but felt certain that a sincere effort was all that was required. I sat quietly and undisturbed. My concentration was sporadic, my attention span childlike. But it was a start.

All the next day, I thought about Dr. Peacock and his request. By dinnertime I was at the computer composing a letter. I thanked people for all they had done so far and all they might be called on to do in the future. But most of all I asked for their prayers, for Remy and for Dr. Peacock and for us as we awaited the surgery, and specifically on that day, which I had just found out would be November 10, five weeks from the day of her seizure. That night I mailed the letter to twenty-five friends and relatives around the country. The next morning I printed and mailed another thirty. The letter was full of intimacy and pain, humility and hope, yet there were only two words that left my fingers on a dare; two words that struck me as a coming out.

"God bless," I wrote in closing. And then I signed off.

15.

full circle

My mother tried to play the part her era and upbringing had assigned her. She married a handsome young executive—a "comer"—and behaved like the loving wife. She joined the Junior League, gave tours of the Music Center, and bought stylish hostess outfits for dinner parties where drinks were not allowed to get low and dinner was rarely served before 10:00 P.M. She had a gardener, a pool man, a hair stylist, a facialist, a caterer, a masseuse, and a full-time live-in maid who gave her children meals and baths and brought them down to say good night to "our guests" in an endearing way. When she was feeling worn down, the doctor gave her a nice fat B-12 shot.

After she left my dad, I spent many a school night in a local piano lounge eating maraschino cherries and hearing about grown-up problems. We went out for just-us-girls dinners. We took just-us-girls trips to San Francisco, sticking our heads out of cable cars and attending spiritual retreats in the woods. On my birthday, we celebrated—just us girls—with sparkling cider and an ounce of green-label beluga caviar, which she let me eat out of the jar with a spoon.

It wasn't until I went out into the world on my own that I realized she had circumvented a great deal of what seemed to be grown-up responsibility. It wasn't until I became a mother that I truly began to resent her moonshiny parenting, creating a rift that was as painful as it was liberating.

God grant me the serenity
to accept the things I cannot change,
the courage to change the things I can,
and the wisdom to know the difference.

THE SERENITY PRAYER, As seen on my childhood refrigerators

Shortly after they found her cancer, my mom rediscovered her love of music. I was told she had been a concert pianist as a teenager, but I had never heard her play. It was Christmastime, just after Graham's second birthday, when she brought out a book of carols and asked me to pick one. I chose "O Holy Night," my favorite for as long as I can remember, and I watched enrapt as her fingers moved across

191

the keyboard like a ballerina en pointe. The sight of them and the sound they made—the ache of tender abandon—were an epiphany.

"Why didn't you tell me?" I asked, dumbstruck.

"Tell you what?" my mother asked innocently.

"That you were an artist."

"Oh, well—I don't know. I do have this gift. I always have. You've heard me play before."

"No. I haven't. Never," I said, stunned.

"Oh, I'm sure you have."

I thought of all the Christmases we might have gathered round for a tune. All the years I had begged to do something old-fashioned and traditional. The time I had asked her to buy chestnuts so I could roast them over an open fire and she brought me a can of chopped water chestnuts with a Japanese label and said, "Gee, I don't really know how it works, honey. I've never done it."

But then I thought of all the holidays to come, for my kids—her grandkids—all of us bundled together like a wreath around the piano bench, singing loudly, badly, the songs of sweet, unjaded joy—*Fall on your knees, oh hear the angel voices*—and that Christmas morning feeling washed over me like the first snow.

It was the day of the Fall Festival at our First Lutheran School of Venice. Very few people had seen Remy since they had started praying for her, both at church and in the weekly school chapel. I had wanted her to be cheery and delightful to put their minds at ease, but she was not. It was hot, and the crowds were noisy and thick. She clung tight to my arms. I was trying to escape the chaos and the obvious concern when someone grabbed my arm from behind.

"Hi, how are you? Gosh, this is so great!" It was Donna, a mom who had been in a playgroup with us when Graham was one. Since then, we'd exchanged maybe a dozen sentences, most of them in a single conversation during a chance meeting at the market earlier that fall.

"Gosh, so Graham's at First Lutheran now?" Donna had said in the checkout line. "We're thinking about sending Hannah there next year. I hear it's great."

"It is. It's wonderful." Donna is an actress, and I figured, *Well, naturally, actress=heathen,* and stepped in to assuage any unspoken concerns she might have. "And don't worry, it's not too churchy."

"Oh. Well, we are. I'm very involved with my church," Donna said.

"Oh," I said, more embarrassed for her than for me.

"I'm hoping other people will be turned off by the church part—make it easier to get in."

"You'll get in. You'll love it. We're having our Fall Festival next month. You should come by. It's a really fun day—good chance for you to see all the kids, get a vibe on the place."

"Okay, sure, yeah," she had said, although I was sure we wouldn't see her there. You know, actress=flake.

". . . and I just met the principal over by the dunk tank," Donna was saying now, plucking a tuft of cotton candy.

"Told him we were very interested in . . ." The moment I met Donna's eyes, my guard dropped, just like the first time I spotted Pastor Ken in our hospital doorway.

"I've got to talk to you," I blurted out.

Kids and balloons and cakewalk music came at us from all sides, but Donna maintained a reverent stillness, holding my hands and crying with me as I told her Remy's story. "I want to come by," she said. "I want to pray with you, if that's okay. We've been doing some amazing healing work at my church and I'd love to just come and be with you—whatever you need."

"Okay," I said in a voice with sound but no air.

An hour after we got home, Donna arrived with a book called *The Healing Light* by Agnes Sanford. "I don't know," she said, "it may seem kind of out there to you, but I really loved it. I mean, it's not some trendy New Age book or anything. It's from the nineteen forties. It was written by the wife of an Episcopalian minister—she was a pretty cool lady, pretty ahead of her time. I had read it before, but we used it again when we did this healing workshop at my church."

"My church." Again and again she said it—*"my church"*—always with pride, fondness, reverence, much the way I would speak of my morning cup of coffee. "So, you know, what church is it you go to?" I asked.

"Oh, it's just a regular old Episcopalian church. It's in Beverly Hills."

"All Saints?" I asked in disbelief.

"Yes. You know it?"

194

"I was baptized and confirmed there. I was married there. My whole family's been going there for years."

"Really? Well, it's a pretty amazing place. You should come with me sometime. There's a Wednesday night service where they do special healing prayers. You want to go?"

I will never know all the mysteries of predestination, but of this I am certain: It was no more random that it was Donna whom I broke down in front of than it was chance that she was there to catch me. The seeds of that day had been planted well in advance, in a scattering of grocery store small talk, three days before Remy's seizure.

Wednesday came, but Donna didn't. She had an audition. So I went by myself, a stranger to the church where I was baptized and confirmed and married, where I had memorialized my father and my grandfather and splashed water on my son.

I arrived just after 6:00 P.M. and managed to squeeze into the very last spot in the very back pew. The hymnals were all taken, so I was unable to sing along. The service was quite structured, with many declarations recited from memory by those who belonged. I surveyed the leaflet but could never find the right spot in time to join in.

Communion was offered. It was one of the few things in the hour-long service I knew how to do; I had learned to do it in that very church. As we rose and lined up to partake of the bread and wine, there was a continuous refrain of a song, "While I am waiting, come," and through that song—through the body and the blood and the standing chest-to-shoulder-blade in line—I began to catch hold of the spirit of the place and thought, *Yes, maybe now, here, of course, the journey comes full circle;* but the service merely ended, and I was left to exit much the same way as I had entered: confused. People chatted in the courtyard, some headed to their cars, others to the parish hall for a dinner of some sort. All possibilities for miraculous encounters were quickly slipping away. And then I turned, just slightly, just a few degrees to the right, and there she was, a woman about my age. "Are you okay?" she asked, noticing my wet cheeks.

"Um, well," I said, "I grew up here. I grew up in this church and my baby's having brain surgery next week . . ."

"Oh my God!"

"Someone said they were doing some kind of healing work or something, so I thought . . ."

"Oh, yes, we're doing amazing things here. You know where the healing rail is?"

"No."

"C'mon, I'll show you."

My life had become like that—*"c'mon, I'll show you"*—like some sort of blind footrace through unknown terrain, and all along the path there were helpers stationed to pass out the one thing I needed to continue, a book or a map or a phrase from a song, doling it out like a swig of Gatorade, then patting me on the back and sending me on my way. And on I ran.

It was a time of small moments and revelation and prayer.

Oddly enough, Remy was not the only thing I had come to pray for—not even the primary thing. I still didn't know if there was some official way to pray, so I started with what I did know, the Lord's Prayer—not some childish, ABC-like recitation, but a thoughtful, mature encounter with the words and ideas, breaking each phrase down and letting it sit. Then, I would thank Him for a litany of recent blessings. Little ones (like the poker-faced Persian nurse who, without prompting, informed her boss that a dressing change on the neck of a baby Remy's age was a challenge for even the most experienced nurse, and that the home health service should take care of all of them for me) and monumental ones (like Dr. Vasquez's wise request for a consult on Graham's murmur from a pediatrician thirty years her senior; distinctive, he said, yes, quite, but not that unlike the good old benign, nonthreatening, and quite possibly temporary variety).

Each hour, each day, my prayer life became more my own, and I would use the time to talk with God about my own struggles and weaknesses, to thank Him for a lifetime of good and great things, to ask for guidance in fulfilling His calling for me. And then it would come to me in a panic, "Oh yeah—and please, God, watch over my little girl now and throughout her surgery and keep Dr. Peacock's hand steady and keep Remy . . ." The words would always trail off . . . *yada, yada* . . . because it was made clear to me again and again: *She is fine. She is well. It is handled. Move on.*

It was all so unexpected. But for those ten days that bridged the moment of grace till the moment of knowing the

197

outcome we would live with, I felt more relaxed, more joyful, more swelled with life than ever before. Perpetual comfort was provided by our close-knit street, an eclectic mix who had come together through raging fires, dead pets, broken marriages, first steps, shortages of flour, surpluses of cake and now this—*oh dear God, not our little girl*—we would go through this together, too. Help was offered in abundance, and I accepted gladly. Calls poured in from friends around the country and, absolved by circumstance, we dared to talk of meaningful things, and of God.

In fact, despite all the syringes and the setbacks and the limbo, there was only one true, dark spot.

The vision. The Boot.

It was more brownish now, the toe less pointy, the clamor more distant. Agnes Sanford described thoughts like these as "residues of past fears," and I sensed that this was true because the images were no longer sent to me from Remy—she was no longer present when they occurred. But still they came, hard and fast, and at least once a day.

Unable to ignore them or pray them away, I decided to work with them, transforming the relentless wallop into all sorts of wonderful things: cymbals clashing, proclaiming triumphantly the success of the surgery; angels swooping down and caressing the growth like fragile treasure, lifting it from the membrane like tape from wrapping paper you intend to reuse, and cupping it till it turned to dust; ballerina fairies, curling up into hard, tight balls, then bursting forth, unraveling Remy's tumor like a skein of golden thread as they ascended, up, up, up, waving the satin strands like banners at some celestial parade. I even toyed with the clamoring sound, adjusting it until it mirrored the *thud-thud-thud* of the MRI, and fathomed that the vision had become a prescient snapshot.

"We'll take another MRI right before the surgery; a 3-D one. Who knows, maybe the growth'll have disappeared," Dr. Peacock had said. "These things happen, you know."

"These things happen," my mother had said with the cool ease of an inside trader, "all the time."

The 3-D MRI took place two days before the surgery. Lon and I arrived in the waiting area of the UCLA radiology department around ten in the morning. There was another couple there, dressed in the same J. Crew catalog wear that was the mainstay of our wardrobes. They were reviewing notes on a legal pad and making relaxed chatter. The woman's parents were there, too, a striking older couple, well-heeled and gracious, sitting next to a Lion King suitcase and a stuffed dalmatian so large it needed its own chair. *Just look at all the nice people who have kids with things growing in their brains.* Remy and I took a seat next to the father. He coughed several times, wiping bagel crumbs from his beard. In a flash he became the enemy.

"You're not sick, are you?" I asked, tilting Remy's face into my chest and attempting to smile.

"No, just a catch in my throat."

"Oh, good. Sorry, but you know, when you've got surgery coming up, you can't be too careful."

"Oh, no, I understand," he said, and I relaxed. *He knows, he understands.* Their four-year-old daughter had finished her MRI an hour before. She was sleeping off the sedative in the observation room, the same room where Lon had taken Remy to have a new IV inserted for her drugs and contrast dye. She was not allowed to breastfeed, so I stayed away. The mother of the four-year-old girl was a tall, slim, serious woman so similar to me in type and appearance that I started to question the genetic corollaries between ectomorphs and brain problems in offspring.

"Your daughter is just beautiful," the chic, silver-haired grandmother said.

"Thank you."

She couched her next question in a nervous smile. "You said she was having surgery?"

"Yeah, she has a little cysty thing in her head. They're going to take it out on Thursday." I told her the whole story, certain that it was similar in many ways to their family's ordeal. "So," I said, ready to hear their version, "your granddaughter is checking into the hospital after this?"

"Oh, no," she replied, discreetly aghast.

"Oh. I saw the suitcase and everything. . . ."

The ponytailed mother in the slim jeans and the sage-colored cotton sweater looked up from her legal briefs. "We didn't know what to expect or anything. We were so nervous about the MRI so we just let her pick all her favorite toys and stuff to bring with her."

I suppose because their daughter was older, or maybe because they seemed so relaxed, I had assumed they had been doing this for a while, or longer than me, anyhow. "Oh, so this is your first MRI?"

"First and last," the father chimed in.

"They already told us she's fine. She's been having headaches and they wanted to check. The doctor came out during the test to let us know, there's nothing there."

"Oh. That's great. That's wonderful. I didn't know they came out and reported back right away like that."

Another young woman, who had been quite emotional and keeping to herself ever since her anesthetized infant had been carried past en route to somewhere, suddenly joined in. "Oh yeah, they came out and told me a few minutes ago. They thought my son might have some sinus blockage, but he's fine. Thank God."

"Oh, good. Great. That's wonderful."

"I'm so relieved," she added breathlessly. "This was the hardest day of my life."

Lon came out to say they were having a problem finding a vein and Remy was hysterical. This was hardly news; I'd been listening to her scream for half an hour. They decided to let her suckle for a bit to calm her down, and so I was called in. I held her lips to my skin. The four-year-old girl in the next bed stirred. Her parents scooped her up in their arms; they made plans to go for a Happy Meal and to watch her *Aladdin* video—"three times, okay, Daddy?"—and they wished us well. By the time Remy was sedated all the kids had come and gone. A gaunt, jumpy woman was now sitting in the bed opposite Remy's. She had been through extensive chemotherapy and stiffened like a child at the prospect of someone yet again searching for a good vein. "No, not there—no, that one's shot. No, it never works in the foot. No, please . . ." She started to cry. A gurney arrived for Remy, and she was wheeled down to the MRI room. Lon was by her side and would stay that way throughout the procedure. I had made other plans.

When our presurgical administrator first suggested I donate a unit of blood, I assumed it was for Remy. It never crossed my mind that our blood types wouldn't be the same or that the request had been made because, in light of the circumstances, kicking in a pint to the general pool might just be the decent thing to do. Donating blood was not something I did, not something I even considered during my sincerest flings with altruism. My dread of needles bordered on the pathological. Remy, as it turned out, was O-negative—a match to neither Lon nor me—and one of the least common types. "Me, me, me! I'm O-negative," said Lynne, Remy's godmother, when I started calling around in search of a match. "Use me, use my blood."

So, technically, our unit was present and accounted for. Technically, I was off the hook.

The volunteer led me into a big open room where I saw five people reclining in huge, padded lounge chairs. Hanging beside them were clear plastic bags filling with fluid that was not in the least bit red or smooth—it looked more like melted butter left to clot.

202

across the room in the platelet section. She wore a purple nylon jogging suit, but was by no means athletic-looking; she was ripe and full-figured, flashing an ivory smile at every nurse who came to check on her and asking how soon she could resume exercise even as the curdled yellow platelet cream was being skimmed out of her veins. Later, we ended up in the lounge together, waiting out our mandatory rest and cookie time. When I asked her why she donated blood, she said, "Oh, someone admired my platelets one day, so I figured, hey, if the good Lord gave me these wonderful platelets, it's the least I can do." Then I asked her to pray for Remy, and I knew when she said she would, she meant it.

As I rode the elevator back down to the basement, I allowed for the off chance that my mom was right, that God had intervened early and I would return to find Lon saying, "You're not going to believe this. . . ." But it was not to be. No one came out to give us a preliminary result of any kind.

That night, on the eve of our hospital check-in, Graham asked to watch home movies. We had taken a lot of video over the past few months and had never had a chance to look at it. Susan Smith, the mother from South Carolina who had driven her two boys into the lake and then blamed it on an African-American carjacker, had just been arrested that week, and as I watched Remy and Graham playing King of the Pillow Pile in Technicolor, I couldn't help thinking of the clips of those two little boys playing on the floor with their mom. Home movies had taken on an ominous tone in recent years, the last memory of a life snuffed out before its time.

The phone rang. "Hello," I whispered, still trying to catch every delicious snatch of noise from the screen.

"Mrs. Davis? Hi. This is Nora—Dr. Vasquez."

"Yes?" I said, and stopped breathing. "What is it?"

"I just called to let you know that you and Remy are really in my thoughts. I just wanted to wish you well and to say God bless you all. You're such a nice family. My daughter and I have been praying for her every night at bedtime. We'll be saying a special prayer here at the office on Thursday."

I returned to the couch, to the candied images of Remy and Graham playing peekaboo. It was impossible not to wonder if these were the last pictures we'd ever have of her; the last shots of joy in this house.

We kept the kids up late that night. There would be time to pack in the morning.

16.

l'chaim

I had asked the hospital for a private room and they had said—two days before the fact—no problem. For an extra seventy-five dollars a night, the sanity would be well worth it. I didn't want to make any new friends. I didn't want to worry about anyone else's children. I didn't want to negotiate politely over the nightly sitcoms. I wanted to be left alone to take care of my daughter, and I had clung to the promise of a private room like the last pillow on a red-eye.

"I'm sorry, but we are full up. There is not an empty bed on the floor. We actually have a child who's been down in

Emergency for six hours—we can't even find a place to put her."

"But you told me I could have a private room. You promised."

"I'm sorry, but there isn't a bed to be had. We won't even be able to place Remy *anywhere* for a couple of hours."

"But you told us to be here at noon."

"I'm sorry. These things happen. It's just impossible to gauge. Here—here are some vouchers for the cafeteria. Go have a nice long lunch, check back with me in an hour or two."

Remy was as ebullient as I was mopey. Sparks seemed to fly off her in all directions, and heads turned her way as if on cue. People approached, one after another, to touch her hand, to earn a smile, to be a part somehow of whatever it was she was giving off. Even the stone-faced doctors and burned-out nurses looked up from their trays and smiled. An old gentleman sitting across from us couldn't contain his admiration. "That's the most beautiful child I've ever seen. Can't be anything wrong with her."

"She has a little cysty thing in her head—gonna have some surgery tomorrow. Then she'll be fine," I said.

"Oh dear God, not this angel. She looks so healthy."

"She is. She's perfectly healthy. She just has a little thing that has to come out." Remy bounced off Lon's lap, playing to the crowd, and I realized then what I was most afraid of: that she would somehow lose this spark, become wooden, or dull, or worse.

My dark thoughts were interrupted by a ten-dollar bill.

207

"Buy her a rattle for me, would ya?" said the old man. "Tell her it's from Eleanor—that's my wife. She died three years ago." He handed me his wallet, flapped open to a picture. "Wasn't she a beauty? Sang for the Metropolitan Opera—voice like an angel. We never had any kids."

Normally, the words *Oh no, I can't take your money* would have jerked out like a reflex. "Thank you. That's really sweet of you," I said instead, tucking the bill in my pocket.

"I'm a born-again Christian, and I believe in the Lord Jesus Christ and in His power to heal. I'm going to be praying for her."

A year before, six months before, six weeks before, even, I might have wiped the bill for cooties. But that day I smiled. "I appreciate it. God bless you."

"You buy her that rattle now, okay? Tell her it's from Eleanor." The small, hunched man tipped his hat and was off, leaving me in better spirits for the encounter.

I scanned each doorway for clues. In one of these rooms lay a sick child and a sick child's family whom at any moment I would have to accommodate. Remy gnawed on her new pink piggy shake toy as I peered in at two Hasidic Jewish ladies in black felt beret-like caps. There was something reverential about them. The admissions assistant continued to lead us down the hallway and I followed her, now bemused. I knew she was going the wrong way. I knew that the room we just passed was the room where we would ul-timately be staying; there was a certain poetry to it. "No, no—the Davises are back there," said the head of admissions to her assistant as she found us several doors down. "Room three-thirty-three," she said. And I smiled. I didn't have to be a theologian to know the perfect symbolism of the number 333.

The women were dressed almost identically, in smart knit suits of bright blues and greens. They wore heavy, flesh-colored stockings and black patent leather pumps, with thick brown bobs well coiffed beneath their caps. Had I seen them anywhere but in this hospital room, I would have assumed they were a mother and daughter heading off to a ladies' luncheon in the city.

"She's having surgery tomorrow, yes?" the older of the two women said.

"Yes."

"What kind of surgery?" she continued.

"Brain surgery."

"With Dr. Peacock?"

"Yes."

"Oh, thank God. He is a saint, that man. He operated on our Mindy two days ago. He's a saint."

"Yes, he is." The younger of the two women did not say a word. *She must be the mother,* I thought. *She must be exhausted, overwhelmed with grief.*

"She has a tumor, or what?" the older woman continued.

"It's a little cysty thing—a lesion."

A nurse was changing the boy's head dressing and I caught a flash of his face from behind the drawn curtain. He was pale, subtly gray, even. There was something not quite right about the way his face and body interacted, but I didn't speculate, although I could have. I could have conjured a thousand and one things, all of them horrid and relevant, but I did not. My mind was still. The older woman stole reciprocal peeks at Remy, struggling to make the pieces fit.

"How did they know? About the cyst?"

"She had a seizure. They found it on the MRI."

"A seizure? Just one?"

"Yes, just one."

"And she was just fine before that?"

"Yep, perfect," I said.

"You must have been a wreck," she said, and meant it. "I can't imagine."

"He's doing okay, you said?"

"Oh yes, he's doing very good, thank you. That Dr. Peacock is a saint."

There was a smell emanating from the other side of the curtain. It had a sickly, rotten-flesh quality that reminded me of the smell of my finger after it had been chopped off and reattached when I was ten. The accident had actually occurred in a gym at UCLA. I had been helping my gymnastics coach adjust the setting on a vaulting horse when my finger got caught in the gap between the sliding metal posts and the entire five-hundred-pound piece of equipment came down on my fingertip like a guillotine. For weeks, my life was permeated by the wretched smell of wet adhesive and excretions gone amok. This is what it reminded me of, the faint smell in room 333.

Two Hasidic gentlemen entered, moving silently past us in their black garments and beards. *These must be the elders,* I thought. *They must be from the council or something. They have come to pray for the boy.* They gathered with the women and circled around the crib, speaking in whispers and not in English—Hebrew, I supposed it was; this ancient rhythmic chant, these soothing foreign sounds. I was glad to have them near me, near Remy. Would they pray for her? I wondered. Did they pray from the same Bible or was it that other thing—the Koran? the Torah? These words came to mind, but I had no idea what they were.

I waited for the wise men to reemerge—to ask them to pray in whatever way they saw fit—but day turned to evening and they did not come out from behind the curtain. One of the neurosurgical residents I had met during our last visit came by. He was handsome, cocky, the only one I had met throughout the whole ordeal who I felt quite certain was in it for the money.

"Well," the resident said, heading out, "we'll see you in the morning."

"Oh, will you be here?" I asked.

"I'll be assisting in the OR."

"Oh," I said, scrambling inside, "well, you better get home and get some sleep."

His parting words were "Don't you worry about me."

And I didn't. God had told me that all was well. Prayers were being said at the base of a dozen bunk beds and up through the rafters of a hundred churches. There was a plan, and if this resident was a part of it, so be it. I returned my attention to my daughter, strapping her into the high chair and serving her a feast of cottage cheese and pears.

From the other side of the room, the prominent sounds of chewing en masse tugged at my ear. It had always seemed to me that food played an important role in the practice of the Jewish faith, and I was curious. I expected to see some sort of holy cloth draped under the meal, an assortment of simple kosher foods methodically placed with regard to meat and dairy and what could touch what on the same plate. I turned around discreetly and found instead a hungry mob ravaging several roasted chickens, bit by bit and bone by bone, grease dripping down every finger, which was then licked clean. There were large tubs of soda slurped heartily through straws and french fries piled up like haystacks. The older woman nodded politely, then returned to her gnawing and smacking beside the identically dressed younger woman and the two black-garmented men; it was then that it struck me that they were husbands and wives—not two weeping women and two men from the council, but two ordinary couples who happened to be Hasidic Jews, the parents and the grandparents of the little boy, no doubt. I could see him now, Mindy. He was sitting cross-legged on the sticky vinyl bench seat that later would become his mother's bed. His head was wrapped in a gauzy turban. There was a certain slowness to his face, but he was laughing merrily and chewing on a drumstick, and his family members all looked as if this was the happiest day of their lives.

It was ten o'clock that night before I finally got Remy down and the black-clad visitors began to file out; first the older man, then the younger, then, to my surprise, the younger woman as well.

"Just you staying?" I asked the older woman when she and I were alone.

"Oh yes, they just flew in from New York this morning—they need to get some rest."

"You came out here alone for the surgery?"

"Oh, before that. We've been here three weeks now. Mindy needed to have his shunt fixed first."

I still had no idea what a shunt was, but I wondered if this was the same shunt Dr. Peacock had left Remy's bedside to fix during our last stay here. I tried to imagine this dignified woman, who I now suspected was not the grandmother but the mother, sleeping all that time on the bench seat while I was home in my own warm bed. "You've been here in the hospital for three weeks?"

"It's not so bad. I like talking to the different people. It's kind of nice. My husband doesn't understand. He thinks I should go stay in a little apartment they offered us here through the temple, but no—I couldn't leave Mindy. I've never spent a night away from him."

"How old is he?"

213

"He's almost four. He doesn't walk or talk yet, but now he'll be able to learn." I struggled to form my next question, but she saved me. "He started having seizures when he was about six months. They never stopped—twenty, thirty, forty times a day he has them. Dr. Peacock started talking to us about the hemispherectomy last year. It took me a long time to decide. As bad off as he was, it's no easy thing to decide to have half of your child's brain removed. There is always some paralysis on the one side. But it was the right decision. Dr. Peacock says the seizures will stop now. Mindy won't be tormented anymore. He can learn. He can have a nice life." She looked over at him, checking. "You have any other kids?"

"Yes, a son. He's five."

"Ah, a boy and a girl. That's nice."

"Is Mindy your only child?" I asked, thinking possibly she'd had decades of fertility problems and was finally rewarded with this.

"Oh no. I have nine children, all grown. All of them perfect, healthy. That was my daughter here earlier. Mindy's my baby. Haven't slept a wink since he was born, but, well, you get used to it."

I stripped off my jeans. The woman looked on unabashedly, and I took comfort in the curious stare of this mother of nine, sitting up straight in her neat knit suit and her patent leather pumps, hands folded, at eleven o'clock at night. The door opened and another woman entered. She was here to see my roommate, although she'd never met her; she belonged to the local synagogue. Contrary to what I was sure were the

214

rules, it seemed they were planning to have a little visit. I turned off the lights on my side of the room and lay stretched out in my recliner. *Rest*. I tried to tune out the voices. *Please, God, let us*— A loud yelp slashed the relative quiet. It was Mindy. At first. Seconds later, Remy began mimicking his cries.

"I'm so sorry," Mindy's mother said from his bedside. "He does this every night. He's not a good sleeper. Is she going to be okay?"

"It's okay, she'll be okay," I said, turning my attention back inward and speaking now to Rem, "it's okay, baby, it's okay, Mama's here, shhh . . ."

It was midnight before I got her back down. The ladies were still whispering in the background, accompanied by a softly played tape of some sort of Yiddish dance music. As I lay there, supremely aware that I was not yet asleep and that Remy would likely be awakened again and again throughout the night, I knew I had been graced with a level of tolerance far greater than my own. I thought of how before—B.C., as it were—I would have stewed over the rudeness of her late-night visitor, the inappropriateness of her playing music and the imperativeness that my daughter get a good rest before her big day—*oh, fuck it*. This woman needs company. *So what if Remy doesn't get a good night's sleep*. This woman needs music. *It's not like Remy has to* perform *the surgery*. I made my peace with the notion of staying up all night—*there'll be other nights to sleep*—as the whispers and the Semitic chants swirled themselves into a holy white noise, which I rode gently into . . .

At 2:00 A.M., the night nurse whom I had befriended on our last visit patted me on the shoulder. "It's time." I nestled Remy to me in the fold-out chair and offered one last feeding but she wanted nothing but sleep; ten minutes later she was back in the crib, and I was alone again. In the dark. The quiet was impaling. I could see my roommate sleeping in the corner, her hair now wrapped in a turban. *Three more hours.* I wanted Mindy to cry out again. *Just three more hours.* I wanted to race to the nurses' lounge, see if they'd let me hang out for a chat. Strangely enough, I did not long for the company of my husband; in that dark hour I wanted only to be with people who were willing to feel the full breadth and depth of the journey. *Dear God, let me sleep. . . .* The door opened a crack and the light spilled across my eyes. The night nurse was coming straight toward me.

"What time is it?" I said, adrenaline held at bay.

"It's almost three. I've got some bad news."

I think I said "What?" but I can't be sure. I was busy making a list: *Dr. Peacock has mysteriously disappeared. They've found something terrible in Remy's lab work. There was something on the MRI that . . .*

"Some of Remy's blood tests were inconclusive."

"What does that mean? Is there something wrong?"

"No, no, it just means that whoever drew the blood earlier today let a few of the vials sit too long. We need to rerun a few of the tests—it's a formality before every surgery."

216

I carried Remy all over the pediatric floor as the nurse and I went in search of the night resident who would have to repoke her. "In the future, you might want to rethink that 'I have some bad news' line," I said, half smiling.

At 5:00 A.M. I awoke like a shot. The room was still and dry as ash. The only sounds in the room were of forced air and breathing—heavy, somnolent breaths, three distinct sounds. I could hear things in the hall now, too. An elevator ding, a cart's wheels, voices growing louder in passing. I registered each sound, each evidence of life, to the hundredth of a second. I tiptoed down to the kitchen for a cup of coffee, taking note of each crack in the floor, each name on each doorway, every detail cast in bronze.

In the shadows of the room I braided my hair and brushed my teeth. I pressed my hands against the warm foam cup and focused, eyes like flood lights, as my baby slept peacefully, knowing nothing. God was with me, but I was not floating on a cloud of otherworldliness. I was present, fully present, hyperpresent. I was Dan Jansen in the locker room, waiting.

They would be coming soon.

17.

limbo

Lon arrived at 5:35 A.M. with a bag of fresh clothes and a drawing from Graham of Pastor Ken holding Remy over a baptismal font. Two men from the surgical floor arrived at six—why, I couldn't say. Her surgery wasn't scheduled until eight-thirty. I asked my Hasidic friend to watch our things. The day we checked into that very room a little girl's brand-new *101 Dalmatians* pajamas had been thrown out while her mother took her down for surgery and the room was quickly readied for us.

"I won't let them touch a thing," she said, bowing her head prayerfully. "God bless you."

I carried Remy down the hall, into the elevator, down to the basement, where everything serious happens. The preop room was a wide-open space with staggered setups for beds to be wheeled into. We were the first to arrive. There was a sterile, metallic chill to the air, an echoey hollowness that did not sit well. Against the back wall there were kids' toys and Crayola-colored wallpaper. A nurse greeted us and led us to a rocker. We sat Remy down and distracted her with playthings she was far too young to comprehend. Patients were wheeled in one at a time, all adults, until the entire room was full, and the empty feeling was absorbed by chatter and cloth. Doctors and anesthesiologists and nurses circled around each one of the patients, discussing, checking, making certain. There was a table in the center of the room — a sort of command central — where the nurse who had greeted us earlier stacked charts, sorted paperwork, collected signatures, and fielded calls. Names were announced from an intercom, papers were checked off and soon the corresponding person was whisked away. It was seven-thirty and still no one had come to see us. My breasts were swelled and obvious to Remy, who was both tired and hungry. Lon held her as I marched over to the desk. "What's going on exactly? What are we waiting for?" I said, trying to be polite.

"Here's the deal. I just spoke with anesthesiology. Dr. Rubenstein had a speaking engagement this morning. He told Dr. Peacock he would be a little bit late. I think they're looking at a nine or nine-thirty start time."

"Well, why did they bring us down here so early? What are we supposed to do with her until then?"

"They probably just wanted to have you here and ready. Don't worry—he'll be here. Really, he's the best with the kids. He's really wonderful. Everything's going to be fine. Let me call again, see if he's on his way."

The assistant anesthesiologist showed up. He was a gentle, fair-skinned man who had been forced to leave his new wife and infant back in Chicago two days earlier to begin this job here at UCLA. He waited with us, talking in a hush that was his full voice, but he didn't have any more information. Nurses came by and helped us keep Remy entertained (this wait would have been harder up in the room, I thought) but she had now been awake and lap-bound for hours and no amount of peekaboo would do the trick. I stormed the command desk again, where the nurse was now sitting beside our lone file.

"He said a half hour. That was fifty minutes ago. What's going on?"

"I don't know. They said he was on his way. I know it's raining, so traffic might be bad."

The assistant anesthesiologist stepped in to listen. My mind started to race. *Is God at hand in this delay? Is He trying to tell me that the ultraexperienced anesthesiologist shouldn't be the one to work on her? Is the sweet new father perhaps the one who will bring her through the danger-fraught fog safely? Maybe the old guy has lost his touch. Maybe he's more interested in the speaking circuit now. Maybe . . .*

"Well," I hesitated, "I mean, how long do we wait? I mean, at what point do we rethink things?"

"That's up to you. Would you like us to request that another anesthesiologist be brought in?"

"I didn't say that," I said like a reflex, buying time. I looked over at the young assistant, scanning for celestial signs. *Do I lie low and let this thing play out as it will, or do I intervene and force it to shift gears? Am I intended to lie low or to act?* I felt like Oedipus trying to outguess his fate. "I was just asking, you know, what the protocol is in situations like these."

The young assistant looked past my shoulder at Lon and Remy in the chair. "She's out."

"Oh, good. The poor sweet baby was so tired," I sighed. "Well, maybe this delay was for the best. Now she can go straight from a nice little nap into the general. That'll make everything easier."

"I wouldn't count on it," the young doctor said. "I've never known a baby not to scream when we take them out of their parent's arms and down to the OR."

The waiting was easier when she was asleep. Her long, fleshy legs were splayed and wrapped around her daddy's waist, her fat pink cheek nestled into his chest like there was no other chest on earth.

"You want me to take her?" I offered.

"No. I've got her," he said, rocking back and forth, back and forth. I looked up at the clock. 9:03. *Let's go, man. Let's get this thing over with.* The surgery, to me, had become something to surmount. 9:05. 9:06. All I wanted now was to get to the other side. 9:10:37, 9:10:38, 9:10:39. A swarthy, round-headed man in surgical scrubs made a penitent entrance, his hands held out like an innkeeper on a small Greek isle. "I am so sorry for the delay. I am Dr. Rubenstein."

"I know. We've been waiting for you for quite a while."

"Please accept my apologies. Dr. Peacock and I have been in communication. He was aware of the delay and will be paged as soon as we're ready. Where is the little one?" She was still sleeping, lulled by the pounding of Lon's heart. "Ah," he continued, "shall we?" I braced myself for her rude arousal, but it was not to be. Dr. Rubenstein scooped her up like a rare archeological find. She never even stirred. Lon and I trailed for a few steps as the young assistant opened the double doors to the restricted hall. He held Remy in outstretched arms—up and out like an offering to the gods—and brushed through them.

"See you on the other side," I called out as the doors swung closed behind them. "See you on the other side," I repeated, squeezing Lon's hand. It occurred to me as I said it that it meant two entirely different things.

I expected the hours to pass like time on ice, every image heightened and tasting of tin and short, dry breaths. I expected to gnaw on the flesh on the inside of my mouth, and roll little paper balls in my fingers, and pace. Instead, I found myself at breakfast with Lon devouring pancakes, weaving conversation out of memories and inside jokes stretching back nearly a dozen years. We laughed until I wept and my belly ached and I gasped for air. There was nothing left to do. We had been delivered into the hands of a surgeon who had pioneered this very surgery and was likely one of the few people in the world who could pull it off. We had loved our daughter well and we had signed on the dotted line. Today God and Dr. Peacock would carry the burden. Today it was out of our hands. Such was the rich, easy feeling of the morning.

My mom and several ladies from her church took turns holding prayer vigil all morning long. Remy's godfather, Greg, hung out for several hours, rubbing my feet and talking with Lon about some new computer graphics software. Donna, the actress, came around eleven o'clock. She wasn't sure she had enough money to get out of the parking lot, but nonetheless she stayed.

"Anyone want a soda? I'm making a run," I asked, rising. I strode back through the lobby and past the clock. 12:51. *My gosh, she's been in there almost four hours. We're more than halfway there.* It was in this giddy daze that I bumped, quite literally, into the cocky young surgeon who was the number-three guy in Remy's OR.

"What are you doing up here?" I said, my voice like clenched fists on lapels.

"I'm getting some lunch."

"Lunch? Now? In the middle of the surgery?"

"We have to eat."

I supposed that was true; I'd just never thought about it. Of course they needed to eat. The nurses and the assistants all should eat, I reasoned. "Well, how's it going in there?"

"It's going fine."

"What do you mean, fine? It's going great, right? She's great, right?"

"She's stable. She's handling the anesthesia well."

"So, I mean, everything's moving along really well, then?"

"They're looking at the tumor now."

The word *tumor* split open my peace of mind like a pickax. *They're looking at the tumor now.* I guess I'd known there would be a pathology at some point—*why now?*—nothing had really changed. *Calm ... peace ... peace of the Lord.* I pictured her comatose and all alone strapped to a table with her brain all chopped up while the gang went out for fajitas. *No. God is with them, with Remy and with Dr. Peacock. He is there. He does not leave the patients. He is still in there,* I told myself, based on nothing more than my need for it to be true. I knew that if the number-three guy got to eat, then certainly Dr. Peacock was entitled to as well, but I couldn't allow it. No. In my mind it was quite clear: All the rest of the team had gone to lunch, but Dr. Peacock was sitting a few feet away from her, watching over her personally and sipping a can of Ensure through a sani-straw. If the truth was something different, I didn't want to know.

For the first time all day, all week even, I battled with the demons of fear. *They are looking at the tumor now.* The real work—the actual shaving away—had not even begun. I needed to be alone. I needed to sleep. I gathered up my pillows and blankets and negotiated the maze of hallways to a remote anteroom with a dozen padded recliners. It was some sort of outpatient waiting lounge, but there was no one in it. The ladies from Pastoral Care had gotten permission that morning for me to rest there. Donna walked down with me. She prayed with me. She helped me up on the recliner, my body suddenly frail, and covered me with blankets against the air-conditioned chill. "I'll call you tonight," she said.

I turned my face toward the plate glass window. The rain had stopped sometime that morning, but it wasn't until now that the clouds began to part and the sun bled through. I nuzzled toward the warmth, praying that I might fall into a blissful sleep. *Why couldn't he have had a bad outcome already? Not recently or anything—not enough to affect his confidence. Just to have it out of the way.* I tried to remember the premise of oddsmaking. *He's only human.* Were the odds the same every time out? Or did the chances increase exponentially? *Just one more. Oh dear God, please . . .* The sunlight won out and I fell into a thick, numb, dreamless sleep, so hard and deep that I couldn't tell minutes from hours, until a grating Bronxy voice shook me like a bum in the lobby of the Ritz. "What are you doing here?"

"What? What time is it?" I slurred.

"You're not supposed to be in here. This is for outpatient recovery only," said the strident young volunteer. "What are you doing here?"

I looked around groggily. There was one other person in the room now—a woman waiting for an arm cast to dry. "I have permission. My daughter is in surgery. What time is it?"

"Who gave you permission?"

225

"The ladies from Pastoral Care. They talked with some-one."

"Who? Who did they talk to?"

"I don't know. What time is it?"

"It's two-ten. I'm going to have to go check on this to see who gave you permission."

"Don't worry about it," I said, realizing I had been asleep for only a few minutes, "I'm leaving, all right?"

I folded my blankets and dragged myself back to the lobby. My mom was the only one still sitting there, watching our things.

"Where's Lon?" I asked.

"A nurse just called up. They said it's going to be a while longer. He went outside for some air. You need anything?"

"I need for this to be over!" I curled up like a potato bug in the tight plastic box-framed chair and buried myself under a blanket. I couldn't bear to pass the time awake. It was exactly then, hidden beneath my gray woolen tent, that I heard it.

"The Davises?"

It was said in a hush to the visitors' liaison thirty feet away on the other side of the bustling lobby, but to me it was like a trumpet blaring straight in my ear. I sprang to my feet. The blankets wrapped around my ankles and tripped me up. I fumbled to a stand, bumping into the coffee table, kicking free the last caught corner of the blanket and moving breathlessly toward him.

"What are you doing here?" I shouted.

"It's out. It's all over. She did beautifully. Fantastic!" said Dr. Peacock, glistening and flushed.

"Oh my God, oh my God. It's out, and she's fine?"

"She's great! They're closing her up now."

"Can I hug you?" I asked, unsure about contaminating his surgical scrubs.

"Absolutely," he said, stretching his arms out and enveloping me. My mom raced in to share the good news. "Go find Lon!" I barked. She hugged me quickly, then rushed outside.

Dr. Peacock sat down and elaborated, "The preliminary pathology revealed one of three things, all benign. The hamartoma. The low-grade astrocytoma. Or possibly, he said, a ganglioglioma—which would be the best of all possible things."

Ganglioglioma, I echoed to myself, *the best of all possible things.* "And they're all benign?"

"All benign. It was a stubborn little mass. At one point I was tugging at it—it was quite literally attached to the membrane—and I really wasn't sure it was going to pull away. I thought I might have to leave a bit of it—that's what I was preparing myself for. And then, I don't know, it just suddenly came loose and lifted right up, clean and easy."

"Really?"

"Yes, it was quite unusual."

My mom reappeared, breathless and contrite. "I can't find him anywhere."

"Listen," Dr. Peacock continued, "I'm going to go check back in downstairs. . . ."

"Go, go," I urged, then added rapturously, "Thank you."

"Thank you so much," my mother said with an extra generation of feeling. My mom and I hugged and cried, and her church ladies hugged and cried. Lynne and Suzie both appeared from somewhere and they too hugged and cried.

"I have to go find Lon." I moved forward as if guided by radar . . . through the courtyard . . . past the benches . . . around the shrubs . . . near the grassy expanse . . . there he was, stretched out on an enormous, elevated utility box, soaking up the sun. "It's all over!" I sang out as I approached. "She's fine. She's great. It's out. They're just closing up."

I lay down beside him on the warm metal platform. He pulled my hand across his chest, smiled his slow, easy smile and said simply, "I knew she could do it."

mer of recognition, each lucid utterance with great hope, but I knew. Mary was gone and she was not coming back. I knew it deep in the heart of where these certainties lie and I mourned her death then, long before her brain stopped sending out the signals to breathe. I had felt the same way about my father. I had felt the same way about my brother. I was absolutely certain that neither of them would ever get better; I never even bothered to wish for it.

By the time Remy underwent surgery, I had come to recognize these unswerving messages of hopelessness as God's way of helping us to prepare. *Look,* He says with a pang. *This is what's happening,* He repeats with a void in your heart where the spark of hope should be. *Open your eyes,* He urges as you try to look away. *Get ready.*

I met up with Lon in the ICU waiting room. He was a captive audience for a mildly high-strung woman in her sixties. I sat down and nodded, smiling, listening, waiting for a break or an introduction or an end to her rambling story—which was not related to kids or illness or urgencies of any kind—but none of these was forthcoming. I looked over at the gray-haired gentleman beside her, certain that at any moment he would tilt his newspaper down and say, "Now, Mother, I'm sure these nice people have their own things to deal with," but he did not. Unable to sit still and listen, I fled to the hallway to stare at the ICU doors.

During our first stay at UCLA, I had stood outside these same double doors and tried to psych myself up. *The next time you're here, Remy will be in that room.* Now she *was* in there, being connected to tubes and monitors and gizmos, and I was no more prepared for what I would see than a woman who's nine months pregnant with her first child is prepared for a real live baby. Each time someone entered or exited the ICU, I craned my neck and peered through the gap in the double doors for a glimmer of my daughter. Finally, a nurse waved me in, and I yanked Lon away from the garrulous older woman in the waiting room. "We can see her now!"

See her . . . my soul raced . . . *see what?* . . . my feet dragged. *Look* . . .

There she was, in the flesh—breathing—her head wrapped in gauze and covered in an elastic, oatmeal-colored stocking cap. Her skin was milky white tinged with a glorious pink; her lips, the deepest red I'd ever seen. She was sleeping beatifically, not a jolt of pain in sight. She looked, as my mom often said, like a Dresden doll. Five weeks after the fact, after the fear and the uncertainty and the sleepless, wretched anguish and the prayers and the faith and the newfound life, we were on the other side. *She made it.* And the other side looked like heaven.

Lon was as happy as I had ever seen him. I leaned into his arms and we exhaled and celebrated our daughter's triumphant journey with a delirious embrace. The double doors opened and I caught sight of Suzie and Lynne and my aunt Anne just outside the entrance. They were huddled together like giggling schoolgirls trying to sneak a peek at something delicious and forbidden, each of them with her hands pressed to her lips as if holding in a secret.

The ICU was cleared of visitors for a shift change. On our

way out, I noticed that there was a curtain drawn around the bed next to Remy's.

"So, what was the deal with that lady in the waiting room?" I asked Lon as I ravaged a turkey sandwich. We had taken our mother lode of homemade treats down to the big family room to get early dibs on two recliners.

"Her granddaughter's in ICU," he replied. "She was born with some sort of major heart problem. She's been in and out of here all her life—had a couple of surgeries, I think. She's eleven months old. They finally thought she might be getting better—she was at home with the family and everything—but then she took a turn, so they brought her back in and, out of nowhere, they find out she has cancer. They never even saw it before. I guess it's pretty bad. She's been in there for a couple of weeks now. They don't think she's going to make it."

I put down my sandwich and sat quietly with the reminder that not all the outcomes are good ones. That God had told me Remy would make it because he knew she would make it; but it is not always so.

The silver-haired grandfather from the ICU waiting room entered just as Lon was heading out to the phones. He took a seat a few recliners down from me. We were the only people in the room.

"Would you like a sandwich? We've got plenty," I said, fumbling.

"No—no, thanks. Appreciate it, though," he said softly.

"How 'bout some pumpkin bread? It's homemade."

"No, thanks."

"Cider? You like cider? My aunt brought me a big thermos of cider, and I have cups and everything," I said, foolishly waving the stack of Styrofoam.

"I'm not very hungry, thanks. I hear your little girl did well today."

"Yeah, she did. She's doing great. We're very blessed."

"Yep, I don't think it's going to be long now for our little one."

This was not the time for platitudes. "Is that what they think?"

"Sweet little thing came in here two weeks ago just pretty as a picture. She's swelled up so bad now we can hardly recognize her. Her body weight has doubled from all the fluid—they can't get the chemo to take, they can't get the swelling down. They're just managing the pain at this point, and I don't even know if that's working for her."

"Is it their only child?"

"No, she has a big sister. She's having a real rough go of it—playing one minute, bawling her eyes out the next."

"How 'bout you? How are you holding up?"

"Well, I'm all right, I guess. God has seen us through a lot, and I know he'll see us through this, too. We lost our oldest daughter ten years back—car accident. She was living up north, and they called us to come up and identify the body, and we had to just sit around the morgue and wait. The car had gone off a cliff and it was raining and they needed a helicopter and some sort of crane to bring her out. My wife didn't go in and look—she couldn't. She's doing better with this, I suppose." I flashed on her rambling and my impatience. "I guess you just get to a point," he continued, "when you've lived as long as us—you have four kids, they have kids of their own—you know in all that, there's going to be hard times. But you also know you get through them. You pray. And nice people like you and your husband listen while we sort things through. We've met a lot of special people here."

A seven-year-old girl was then ushered in by a different grandmother, who looked like she was plumb out of distractions. The little girl stared at her shoes. "I have a little boy at home about your age and he loves granola bars," I said in my best Girl Scout voice. "You like granola bars?" The girl brightened and the grandmother beamed. "Well, let's see here . . . I've got two kinds. I've got strawberry and I've got peanut butter-and-chocolate. Which one do you want?" She eyed them back and forth, a thin smile spreading out over her pale face. "You know what? Why don't you take both of them? Save one for later."

"Okay." She nodded and held out her hand.

"Thank you," the grandmother said.

"Thank you," the little girl echoed.

The door flew open. "Peacock's here!" Lon said excitedly.

I turned back to the grandfather. "I'll be back in a few minutes, okay? I just want to talk to our surgeon real quick."

We could hear the screams from well outside the ICU doors. Inside, Dr. Peacock was leaning over Remy, who was now wide awake and determined to curdle blood. "Does she have a little pacifier from home?" he asked, flustered.

234

"No. She's never taken one. Spits them all out."

"Yes, well, that's what I'm finding." Dr. Peacock had his pinkie in her mouth trying to console her. Remy pounded her fists in the air and reached for the sound of my voice with a desperate lunge. Unsettling as it was, it was ample proof that she was in full control of all her functions. "I want her sedated—now!" Dr. Peacock said with an urgency that didn't soothe. The nurses swooped in, adding sacks of a morphine substitute to her IV and conferring in hushed tones. There were whispers coming from behind the curtain next to us as well.

"I've given an order for her to be sedated throughout the night," Dr. Peacock reported back twenty minutes later. "It's very important that we keep her still—keep the internal swelling to a minimum—especially during this first twenty-four-hour period."

"But she's all right, isn't she?"

"She's too strong for her own good. I suggest you go home, get some rest."

"Well, we were planning on camping out here. . . ."

"I wouldn't. You have a long weekend ahead of you. I'd sleep while you can."

When we returned to the family room for our bags, our silver-haired friend was gone. We drove home talking on a borrowed cellular phone that we plugged into the lighter. I had always hated cellular phones; it seemed to me that somewhere along the line people had started confusing actual productivity with the mere physical connection to anything electronic. When the world news announced that cellular phones might actually cause brain tumors, I remember thinking, "Ha! Serves 'em right, all those ridiculous little monkeys with those black plastic ear pacifiers." But on that night I was thrilled to have one, as I spread the good news from Westwood to Venice, fumbling with the little glowy buttons and leaving behind my days of wishing brain tumors on anyone.

We returned to UCLA at eight o'clock on Friday morning. Remy had been sedated all night and was still asleep when we got there. The curtain beside her was no longer drawn. The bed was gone entirely.

Later that weekend I would see a handmade sign posted on the back of a door in the nurses' area. It said that the funeral for Meghan Rose would be held in Santa Monica that Monday, and although I'd never met her—didn't even know her last name—I wondered if there was any way for me to be there.

19.

this is me

"All right, you can feed her now," Dr. Peacock said, upgrading me from standby to instant terror. By six o'clock Friday night, Remy's face had swollen up like a prizefighter's; one eye was sealed shut, the other barely a slit.

"Now?" I asked. It was painful just looking at her. The nurses eyed me impatiently; I had been hounding them all day about when I'd be able to resume breastfeeding.

"Whenever you're ready," Dr. Peacock answered, then stepped away.

"No. Don't go!" I said. The thought of having to lift her, to hold her, to cradle her head scared me half to death.

"I mean, I want to make sure I'm doing it right." There were two separate IVs wedged into her groin, each feeding into an outlet that branched off into a mane of wires and lines — some for fluids, some for drugs, some for monitoring blood pressure and blood gases and fever. Her lap was like the back of a stereo cabinet. "You're sure I'm not going to disconnect her?"

"It's fine, really," a nurse interjected.

I maneuvered like a bomb squad technician, slipping my fingers beneath her small, clammy back, scooping her up ever so gently and — "hello, sweet angel, please don't move" — draping the wires like a wedding train as I laid her across my lap and pressed her mouth toward my nipple. "Is this okay — like this?" I asked Dr. Peacock, my shirt lifted.

"Fine. Just fine . . . ," he mumbled, backing away shly.

"No. Look! Look at where her head is," I bleated nervously. It seemed to me that to a raw, blood-pounding wound, my bony forearm would feel about as comfortable as the mean seam of a 4x4. "Are you sure this isn't going to hurt her, the way she's leaning like this?"

"No, no . . . that's just fine," he replied, pulling the curtain closed. "We'll see you tomorrow."

She fed well and kept it down, but was not in the least comforted by me or anyone else. She couldn't open her eyes and it made her crazy. Every time she moved a limb, she got tangled up in one wire or another, which triggered a new round of misery and combativeness. And the state of affairs in the ICU only made things worse. Doctors and visi-

238

tors came and went around the clock. Buzzers and beepers and cries for help stole your attention from five beds away. After only a few hours at her side, I was as agitated and overwrought as she was.

A boy close to Graham's age was wheeled in just as *The X-Files* was starting. He was wearing the same oatmeal-colored stretch cap that Remy had on. *Dr. Peacock's Friday hemispherectomy,* I thought. When I stepped out for the 10:00 P.M. shift change, there were two men in the ICU waiting room: a tall, scholarly-looking fellow and an older man—a grandpa—who was a dead ringer for Einstein. They were both beaming.

"Was that your son who just came in?" I asked the younger of the two.

"Yep. Sam, that's Sam."

"So everything went well today?"

"Great, terrific—much, much better than we expected."

Over the next half hour I would learn that Sam had been a strapping, healthy towheaded three-year-old when one day his face began to twitch. It continued for several hours, becoming gradually more severe. His parents took him to the emergency room. By midnight—twelve hours after the very first sign of twitching—the doctors had begun to suspect herpes encephalitis. Acyclovir was a fairly new treatment at the time, but they put him on it immediately. A brain scan done in the wee hours revealed that 60 percent of the left side of his brain had already been totally destroyed. They were not even sure if he would make it through the night. Ultimately, the acyclovir prevailed, but the damage to the brain tissue had left him beleaguered with seizures. His development was thwarted, but he could still run and laugh and play. Twenty or thirty times a day he would just seize, tipping over into his lunch or dropping to the ground in the middle of a game of tag with his baby sister.

"Do they know how he got it?" I asked.

"No, they never do. I was reading a book about it once where a doctor said that, basically, every once in a while—every couple hundred thousand cases or so—a regular old everyday herpes virus will just decide to hitch a ride on a nerve ending and torpedo straight up to the brain. It's just incredibly bad luck." I was speechless. "We've been living with this for so long now—for two and a half years—it's been our life. I guess we've just gotten used to it. You adjust to whatever you're dealt, I suppose. I sort of forget how terrible it is sometimes, until I tell the story to someone new and I look into their eyes"—I would have moved heaven and earth to stop the first tear from streaming down my face, but I could not—"and then," he said with a voice like a sinking stone, "I know." He took off his glasses and wiped his eyes, too.

It had been a very long day.

"Well, the risk of swelling in the brain at this point is very low," Dr. Peacock said on his Saturday morning rounds. "Of course, we will continue to monitor for infection, but she doesn't need to be in the ICU for that. Her range of motion is a hundred percent. I suppose you won't feel totally relieved until you're out of here, but from my point of view, we're out of the woods. I've signed your release onto the floor. As soon as there's a room free, they can move her down."

I hounded the nurses at fifteen-minute intervals, but it did nothing to free up a bed. I was tired of hanging around the ICU. I was tired of the beepers and the nearby death. I was tired. "I need to eat," I said, leaving Lon and my mom with Remy and heading out to the twelve-foot-by-twelve-foot holding cell of a waiting room, which, at present, was crammed like a frat house pay-phone prank with six adults, four children, and a toddler with a soiled diaper. "Hello," I said curtly as I squeezed in toward my pile of stuff, "excuse me."

An enormous gift basket of gourmet muffins had been delivered to us that morning, but I hadn't had a moment to open it. I could feel twenty-two eyes upon me as I parted the crinkly cellophane. "Would anyone like a muffin?" We went through the exercise of them all saying no three times and me insisting and then each of the kids hungrily taking two. The toddler continued to exert more energy than would fit in the space, but no one made any effort to take her out. "There's another waiting room down the hall, you know. It's much bigger. It has a TV and everything."

"We stay here," the patriarch said in broken English.

"I just thought maybe it would be easier for the kids down there—a little more room to move around. They have video games, too, I think."

"We fine here," he said, not smiling.

I skulked back into the ICU and burst. "I know I should

241

be just totally happy and grateful and patient, but fuck, man—I'm sick of it. I don't have anywhere to go. I'm sick of all these people hanging around. I'm tired of this fucking hospital. I've still got at least two more days to go with her here and I'm suffocating. I've had it. I've just had it."

Later, alone, as I sat in the ICU rocker feeding Remy and hating myself for my petulance and ingratitude, I realized, *This is me without God.* I was not at peace, and as if that was not enough of a punishment, I hated myself for not being at peace. I guess I thought that I might feel forever the magnanimous love, strength and inner calm that I had been given over the past weeks, but I was wrong. Grace came to me when I didn't have the strength to go on, but like any good free-trial offer, it expired. After that it was up to me to seek out, to renew and to cultivate a relationship with God.

In the late afternoon, I went down to the chapel and tried to pray. I was restless and unfocused and resentful. There were no epiphanies. There was no peace. *This is the work that lies ahead.*

When I came back from the chapel, they were preparing Remy's bed for transfer. As I lifted her up, she started to bleed—a trickle at first, then a stream, oozing down from her nose. I summoned the ICU doctor, who looked at her quite seriously.

"What? What is it? Is it a problem? Are you worried?" I asked as she flashed her penlight into Remy's swollen eyes.

"I'm not worried right now," she replied.

"What does that mean?"

242

"It means that right now she has a bloody nose, and at this point I am not alarmed by it."

All I could think was that her entire brain was caving in on top of itself and at any moment large bloody clots would start spilling out of her tiny nostrils and I would be grabbing for pieces of them like Jackie in Dallas, cupping her innermost thoughts in my hand and saying, *Look—look!—now will you take this seriously?* Instead I offered, "She just had brain surgery, you know."

"I'm aware of that, Mrs. Davis."

"Well, and now she has blood coming out of her nose, which is originating from God knows where."

"The nasal passage does not connect directly to the brain, if that's what you're asking. The air here in the ICU is very dry—most likely, that's the cause of it."

"And what if it's not?"

"If she continues to bleed for several hours, or more heavily, then I'll call neurosurgery in, okay? Until then, why don't you go get settled on the floor?"

My roommate that night was as displeased to be making a new acquaintance as I was. Her five-year-old son had had a liver transplant as a newborn, and had recently run a high fever and needed to be observed. His sweet, intelligent voice from behind the curtain reminded me of Graham, and I thought how difficult it would be to go through all the medical rigmarole with a child who was old enough to understand it and ask questions. She played Nintendo with him for four straight hours, which, in my book, made her a saint.

*　　*　　*

By nightfall, Remy's nose had stopped bleeding entirely. She was sitting up in her crib in her purple-striped dress with a shiny bald head and a crescent-shaped gauze pad taped over her incision. Friends arrived to visit. They had braced themselves for a deathbed scene but found instead a frisky nine-month-old tweezing raisins from a tiny red box and chomping them down with a juicy smile. You could see it in their eyes, the enormous relief. I too was relieved by the sight of so many good friends. *Perfect.* So many fresh hands to hold her. *This is it!* I knew there would never be a better time to escape. "Great to see you all, really—gotta go," I said, bounding down the stairwell three steps at a time and diving headlong into the cool night air.

I jumped in my dusty van, the stereo blasting as I banked around and down the stone's throw to my grandmother's house. There I was greeted with a whisper of Debussy and a hot, civilized shower. I washed with scented soaps shaped like butterflies and dried off with a towel bearing the combined monograms of my grandmother and grandfather, who'd been dead now for over twenty-five years. It had been raining all day and the house was filled with soft, napping heat. I slathered lotion all over my dry, hospitalized skin and lay stark naked on top of the antique canopy bed, paralyzed with exhaustion. The maid brought me in tea and cookies and my grandmother followed on her heels with the Neiman Marcus catalog.

"Don't you want to cover up, sweetie? You'll catch your death."

"No, I'm fine, thanks. It feels good, really."

"Well, all right, then," she said, biting her tongue. "I brought you this—they have some lovely things. Why don't you look through and see if there's anything you like in here?"

"Thanks."

"You sure you don't want me to cover you up?"

"No, that's okay. The air feels good, really."

"Okay. All right. If you need anything, just ring."

She tiptoed out and shut the door. The silence wrapped around me like a fur. *It's nice to have someone make you tea and cookies and deliver them on a tray to your bed. It's quite lovely to be surrounded by fine wood and silk pillows and ornaments collected from around the globe. It is seductive to visit a place where the illusion is so well maintained.* A chill crept over my skin, and I got under the covers, thinking about my grandmother. Thinking of how my lying here naked in front of the maid must have embarrassed her, but she had fought the urge to disapprove. She had tried—for me; she had tried. I was not her daughter. I was once removed. She didn't understand me, not in the least, but she never let a visit pass without telling me what a wonderful job I was doing with the kids, what a beautiful marriage I had made for myself, how proud she was of me. She bought Lon his first computer so he could start up his own business at home. She would cancel anything for the chance to drop her eighty-five-year-old frame to the floor and roll around with my kids, more often than not calling Graham "Michael" and proving once again, as if we needed any more proof, that life carves no memory more lapidary or indelible than the years shared with young children. And she had waited, delicately trembling, to hear the outcome of my daughter, heralding the good news with a charming gasp, a lilty society trill, born of another era, cultivated for a lifestyle that became obsolete shortly after she and others had elevated it to an art form. "I love thee," she said at the end of that visit and others. And I fought the urge to remind her that we were living in California, in this, the twentieth century.

I was back in Remy's room an hour and a half later, restored and companionable, clearer still on how God answers prayers. Through a cup of tea, a warm bed, one small hand carrying you from here to there as needed. I have come to see that these—us, we—are his tools.

20.

thank god for small nightmares

In the morning, the five-year-old boy in our room needed his blood drawn. A timid-looking Asian woman with a lab tray disappeared behind the curtain. I heard murmurs of tension but didn't understand them. The boy was whimpering. Finally, his mother blew, "That's it! That's six tries. You get it this time, lady, or you're out of here."

"It's not my fault. He's too wiggly. He's got bad veins."

"My kid's got great veins. No one's ever complained about his veins. You've got one more try and that's it. So get it right this time." I sat behind the curtain, waiting for the other shoe to — "You get the hell away from my kid! You are the worst fucking phlebologist I've ever seen. You get out of here *now*!"

Her son was crying and screaming. The lab lady was shouting as she backed out the door with her tackle box of test tubes and rubber cords, "You not nice lady. You mean lady."

"You haven't seen anything yet, you bitch. Come in here and poke my kid seven times—seven fucking times—and you get shit. I'm going to report your ass—you'll never come up on this floor again if I have anything to say about it. Now, get the fuck out of here!"

Nurses were gathering in the hall, eyeing me for answers. I was speechless, not because of the woman's ire, but because of the thought of what she must have lived through to be able to utter the words "worst fucking phlebologist" with such conviction. She jutted her head out from behind the curtain and glared at me. "I know you're sitting there thinking I'm some kind of psychotic bitch."

"No. I'm not, really." I shook my head and rose, speaking in a hush over Remy, who was, inexplicably, sleeping through it. "We're not here to be popular."

"Damn straight."

The angry mom and her son were released with a clean bill of health later that day. I went down to the chapel and prayed for my own peace of mind, for Remy's continued healing, and for no new admissions that night. We only had one more day to go and I didn't think I could survive another roommate. I got everything I prayed for but the peace of mind.

Every blood pressure reading, every temperature taken, every resident who looked into Remy's eyes and took notes on their findings wound me up a little tighter. I saw every whimper as the threat of a setback. The left side of her head had tripled in size overnight. The tissue was so engorged that her ear stood out from her head at a full ninety-degree angle.

And there was that smell, the same rank odor that came wafting from Mindy's postoperative head. I found myself looking at Remy, gagging at the sheer force of the bulging, throbbing mound, sniffing her like a dog, checking for pus or inappropriate redness, conjuring infection from every angle. We paced the halls. I grew more maniacal, formulating scenario after scenario. I passed a group of doctors consulting in the hall; the word *neurosurgery* screamed from a name tag and flagged me down. I crashed their tight, somber circle like a wrecking ball. "Smell her head, would you? What does that smell like to you?"

The rather stunned doctor took a whiff. "It smells like the tape we use to hold the sutures flat."

"Oh. Good. Thanks," I said, mildly relieved, free to concentrate my anxiety now in other areas, which was easy. The halls were packed. Germs seemed to be congregating outside every doorway. Families spilled out from the waiting room, moist with grief and concern. I buried Remy's face against my chest as we moved quickly past the breathy mobs. It felt like we were no longer recovering patients, but hostages in a breeding tank of disease.

By early evening, Suzie arrived with take-out Chinese

and a little perspective. "It's almost over. You'll be home tomorrow," she said.

"It doesn't feel like it. Every second we're stuck here it feels like we're never going to get out alive—like any minute someone's going to walk in and go 'uh-oh' and it's going to start all over again."

"Nothing's going to happen. She's great. She's wonderful. Every time I walk her around, people come up to her and are just totally shocked that she had brain surgery three days ago. I mean, it's only been three days, and look at her."

"What about all this swelling?"

"It's just swelling—normal, healthy swelling. She's wonderful. You're wonderful."

"I'm a basket case."

"You know, when I first got the call about the seizure, I ran home and got under the covers and thought, 'This is why I never want to have kids.' But now, going through it all with you, seeing you and Lon together, now I want them more than ever."

"*This* has made you want kids?"

"Yeah."

"Really?"

"Really."

"It has been pretty amazing."

"Yeah. It has."

"You'll have them," I said to my friend of twenty years. "You'll find someone wonderful and it'll all come together."

"Maybe," she said, her eyes flitting to some unfixed point on the floor.

"You will," I said, at peace again for the first time in hours. "I'll be praying for it."

On Monday morning Dr. Peacock made his rounds and signed our release, just four days after Remy's surgery. His visit was short; there were new patients down the hall, new tumors and ills and seizure-ridden brains. We were on the verge of becoming outpatients and I was reluctant to say good-bye.

"Yes? Is there anything else?" he said in response to my longing expression.

"Well, could you just say, 'Heather, it's all over. Remy is fine. You can close the book on all this and go home and have a wonderful life'?"

He looked at me quite sternly. "Heather, it's all over. She's fine. You can close the book on all this and—" He stopped and smiled. "What was the last part?"

"Go," I said, and hugged him. "Go next door. They're really having a tough time. They've been waiting all weekend to see you."

I had met the aunt of the girl next door two nights earlier. She told me that her seven-month-old niece had been having daily seizures for the past several months, and even though an MRI had revealed a tumor of some sort, it was not in an area that should have been causing seizures. They would not declare her as a neurosurgical patient until they could prove a correlation. This baby had been hooked up to about a hundred different wires and probes round the clock for five days while the entire department waited for a single telltale tie-in. There was not a twitch.

Once more I was reminded of the magnificent simplicity of our family crisis. One fluky bug that brought on a temperature that triggered a seizure that lasted just long enough to cause some paralysis, just enough to look further, just enough to find the tumor—a tumor perfectly matched by the EEG to the location of the seizure. We were blessed to have switched, only months before, from a tightfisted, red-tape-dispensing HMO to one that, in tandem with the doctors from our new medical group, handled every single step with astonishing professionalism, care and uncompromising coverage. Through them, it was one swift and easy transfer right into the hands of Dr. Peacock, a surgeon others had traveled continents to see.

In someone else's crisis, Dr. Peacock may not have come so easily. Their journey may have required research and digging and phone calls and moving mountains, but God knew I didn't need any work in that area—I would have plowed through all of that with glee. Someone else's journey may not have needed the encephalitis decoy, but mine did. God wanted me tired and uncertain, forced to face my dread of germs and fatal diseases, and humbled by tasks that were precise and repetitive and gave no points whatsoever for creativity. In someone else's journey, a child might have had to suffer more. For that I have no answer, only ceaseless gratitude that God kept Remy's suffering to a minimum. Two days after the surgery she needed nothing more than the occasional dropper of Tylenol. Two weeks after the surgery, the stitches came out, revealing a swooping crimson-stitched scar that made her bald head look, rather amusingly, like a baseball.

Still, the at-home recovery period was not all green grass. A baby's skull takes six weeks to heal completely. "I've never had a patient return with a collapsed skull plate," Dr. Peacock had said in an attempt to put our minds at ease.

We took every imaginable precaution: We removed all mean-cornered furnishings. We dropped her crib mattress down to the lowest setting and propped one end up to help reduce the swelling. We padded our slate coffee table with a doubled-over comforter duct-taped around all sides; none of it was comfort enough. Every time Remy made a move, we were right there behind her, bracketing her neophyte cruising motions as if gauging the size of a fish.

At night, she awakened frequently; whether it was bad dreams or pain or merely a break in routine, we'll never know. Fortunately, Graham was a very sound sleeper; parties, sirens, screaming sister, he slept through them all. In his five-plus years, he woke only a handful of times, which is why it was so startling to see him at my bedside at 4:01 A.M. just weeks after the surgery. "I had a nightmare. I had a nightmare that Rem was on a high, high—" Before he could finish the sentence I bolted upright.

"C'mon, baby," I said, scooping him up, jogging him back into bed, tucking him in with a quick rub and a kiss and racing next door. I opened it, breath held, to find the crib rail all the way down to the floor. *Oh dear God.* I raised it up ever so slowly and returned stupefied to my bed, doubting, at 4:03

that morning, as I never had before in my life, my own competence. *I can no longer be trusted with her safety.* This was the truth I stared at in the dark till my thoughts were interrupted by a shriek at 4:06. I ran back to her room and found Remy standing up, screaming, gripping the top of the crib rail that just three minutes before had not been there.

The proof had become so overwhelming it was getting to be downright scientific. Where I had fallen dangerously short, God had intervened, preventing Remy from tumbling to the hardwood floor, her jigsawed skull plate caving in like a watermelon tossed from a skyscraper.

21.

blood and gratitude

People called often over the next few weeks. They hesitated before asking, but they always asked, "So, uh, did the final pathology report come back all right and everything?"

"Oh," I would say, surprised, "I don't know. They said it takes a week or so. I'll find out when we see Dr. Peacock next month for a checkup."

For the first time in my life, I did not worry about a lab result, about the possibility that the doctors had been wrong or that the growth may have been atypical. I started writing this book and I titled my computer file GANGLI, in honor of the ganglioglioma that I had come to feel certain she had. "Hmm, let's see here ...," Dr. Peacock said, flipping through the paperwork at Remy's one-month checkup. "Yes, here we go . . . ganglioglioma. Fabulous."

"The best of all possible things," I said.

"Yes, well, I say that because it's a developmental anomaly, the result of two brain cells—opposites, really—that are designed to collaborate in the growing process, but which in Remy's case decided to butt heads and form our little knot." I imagined these obstinate cells in a power struggle for the tenor of my daughter's fetal brain. "It's really quite rare. And I've never seen a case of it recurring—I don't believe one even exists in the literature. With the other growths we discussed, there is always the possibility, however slight, of recurrence. With those, I would have recommended a yearly MRI, well . . . indefinitely. But with the ganglioglioma, we'll check her for a few years, then I think that'll be enough."

"Really?" I said, instantly processing the difference between two or three toddlerhood MRIs versus MRIs, like Pap smears, for life.

"Yes. As long as she continues to progress well neurologically, which she certainly is doing now, and as long as she remains seizure free—which I have no reason to believe she won't—I think this will be a case of looking back and saying, 'We certainly won't forget her first year of life.'" We all turned to watch Remy scaling a step stool and stopped for a beat. *Small miracle.*

As we drove home that afternoon, I found myself thinking about opposites, about pairings—more specifically, about paradox. I had been reintroduced to the concept of paradox in the book *Further Along the Road Less Traveled,* by M. Scott Peck. The book was a gift from Graham's principal, with whom I'd exchanged the occasional cryptic comment about the search for deeper meaning. I was sitting on a bench at school one day when he approached. "Here," he said, "I think this might speak to you," then walked away.

I had actually read Peck's first book, *The Road Less Traveled,* years before and enjoyed it, although the only thing that stuck with me from the entire text was the notion that people who are mildly neurotic usually make excellent parents because they tend to be so responsible.

In his follow-up book, he addresses many of the roadblocks I had faced, such as faithlessness disguised as devoutness and "evil" done in the name of God. He described in personal terms "the grace of breaking moments" and the importance of preparation. He even spoke of *Atlas Shrugged,* saying it is "a book that so compellingly puts forth a philosophy of rugged individualism and unrestrained self-interest that I was tempted to convert to being a right-wing Republican . . . , [Then], I realized that in this panoramic novel of almost twelve hundred pages there are virtually no children. Children were missing. Of course, that's exactly where Rand's philosophy . . . begins to break down—with children and people in our society who need other people."

Ultimately, his writings put the "Jesus thing" within my jaded grasp by suggesting that paradox—the paradox of Jesus, both fully human and fully divine—is at the core of it all.

What had once seemed to me to be little more than a puppet show came to strike me as both the thorniest and most liquid truth of all.

I could chant on a hilltop till I'm green in the face, but I will never transcend my humanness. I could turn my back on all things unprovable but still never escape my divinity. I will always be, simultaneously and in mercurial proportion, both contented and wanting, teacher and student, peaceful and wretched, responsible and powerless, earthbound and heaven-sent—no more or less than Jesus himself—and it is in the embrace of these poles, and in the surrender to this truth, that I can find peace.

"A house divided against itself cannot stand"—so sayeth the Gospels. Here ends the lesson of ganglioglioma.

Remy was baptized a month after the surgery. I had fantasized that day like the opening scene from *The Lion King,* where she would be lifted before the congregation who had prayed for her so long and so well, and I would be swept up in weepy, orchestrated ecstasy. Instead, Lon and I tried to contain a healthy, restless ten-month-old festooned in white chiffon and satin bows through the longest service in history as the schoolkids sang Christmas songs and Pastor Ken gave a sermon on Christmas memories and a seemingly endless parade of Christmas candles were lit by wobbly acolytes and Greg the godfather read from the Scriptures and Lynne the godmother read from Gibran and Remy bounced and bobbed and squirmed and wriggled and flopped and chewed on the hair of the kindergartners sitting in front of us, yanking at the toes of her little white tights, quieted only by a quickly diminishing supply of all-natural corn puffs. By the time we rose for the baptism itself, I was a sweaty, frazzled mess, nodding in agreement to everything that was said and quickly passing her off to Lynne, who let Remy splash in the baptismal font to keep her quiet while the liturgy was completed.

I remember hearing only one sentence of the entire sacrament. "Remy was doubly blessed," Pastor Ken said, addressing the overspilled church, "having been healed by the hands of a great Christian surgeon, and born into the arms of a great and loving Christian home," and at that I stopped dead and realized he was talking about us.

I moved out through the congregation, through the wide-eyed children who had prayed for "the baby with a problem in her brain" every Wednesday in chapel and wanted, now, to hold her. I was approached by new mothers who looked both delighted and wary, and aging men who had done their time in hospital waiting rooms. I was embraced by ladies born into a generation of service who, without ties or hesitation, sent us cards and casseroles and Jell-O Jigglers for Graham, and I was grateful to have a place in all of their lives. Church, as I have been blessed to discover, is not boot camp. It's a place to practice being a human being.

The blood donor center calls me every sixty days, and I go. I give blood out of gratitude. I give blood to remember . . .

when it all changed, why I came to believe, what it was like when I didn't, what it was like to be afraid.

I read the Bible now, too. Oftentimes it's as visceral as poetry. Other times I'm forced to accept that there may be words or passages that just don't sit right and never will. Like people clinging to the notion of "being saved." (Faith, I am quite certain, was not meant to be bought into like life insurance.) Or prayers that call for the demise of "nonbelievers." (If I have learned anything, it is that each one of us—each us, each them—is only a day, a birth, a breath, a death, a disillusionment away from seeing things differently.) I still wince at words like *evil* and *sin,* but I realize now that it's all semantics. I can call a tumor a cyst if I want, but it won't change the nature of the beast. So it is with sin.

My grandmother gave Remy a cross for her baptism. I put it on a long chain and have yet to give it back. It occurs to me that people look at me differently when I wear it—like I have looked at them in the past—and I laugh at my former foolishness. I know now that nothing so deliciously complex as a human being could ever be so superficially defined, and yet we try. I suppose it makes things easier.

Certainly, it would be easier for me *not* to go back to a religion I had already rejected. Easier *not* to struggle with reconciling what was put forth to be life-affirming with the racism and hypocrisy it has so often spawned. Easier just to take my healthy daughter and backstep down to a safe, hip attitude of urban agnosticism and forget the whole thing.

But I've never been impressed with easy. And I have no interest in forgetting.

My life has been littered with the bodies of men who could not find God. I do not intend to join them. I have found my words to live by. My big brother to talk things through with. My bosomy grandma to embrace. The cracks in my psyche don't need to be filled with TV or wine or someone else's shortcomings. They can be filled with God's extraordinary power, seeping in like spinal fluid in my daughter's brain, infusing the tunnels and fissures, making connections, bridging the gaps and, with time, I pray, making the pieces expand and grow till they touch all the way around in a perfect circle.

I have a world of things to do, but I no longer make big plans. If I'm needed for anything in particular, I trust He'll get my attention.

God, in my experience, is pretty good about stuff like that.

You have shown me the paths that lead to life,
and your presence will fill me with joy.

ACTS 2:28

I said there were three dreams. This is the third one. It came shortly after Remy's follow-up MRI, taken two months after the surgery. It showed that the tumor had been completely excised and nothing had returned.

I am flying. I know that it's common for people to fly in their dreams, but I cannot remember doing it before. My body is draped in silky white cloth and I have white feathered wings that span out and keep me weightless and aloft. The clouds are white-hot and startling, like kicks of sunlight off in the desert, and I am soaring, not just high, but fast, speeding, racing, peeling back the clouds, and I am singing, shouting, booming the gospel of "Amazing Grace," which I have never sung before and was not aware I knew the words to, but now I sing, soaring, flying, parting the sky with Mahaliaesque perfection. The voice is mine—not one I have ever heard or used before, but nonetheless wholly mine, bellowing, bursting, reverberating till my chest begins to vibrate and swell, air and voice and soul as one, taking flight and gliding, sailing, rising up and—

"Ama-mamaa!" Remy calls out, and I bolt upright, pressing my hand to my chest. My heart is pounding. My lungs are tingly and hot. I am nearly short of breath. And although it is early—too early—I smile.

And give thanks.

acknowledgments

My dear friend Rob Jennings once said to me, "Heather, you're always happiest when you're writing, or when you've just finished writing — everything else about the business makes you crazy." For the most part, he's right. But the experience of bringing this book from unsold manuscript to publication was made far less painful by three people: My insightful friend and neighbor Jacob Conrad, who, when asked if there was such a thing as an agent who was both good and decent, made a very short list, and at the top of it, put the name Jonathon Lazear, who has proven to be just that; and Emily Heckman, my editor at Bantam, who helped me fine-tune this manuscript with clarity, vision and uncompromising standards, and in doing so, led me gently toward the book I set out to write.

There are many others who have supported my work, my spiritual growth and my family. I'd like to thank Lisa Gorneau Wynkoop and Christine Kellogg Darrin for their generous proofing and critiquing of the early drafts. Dr. Pamela Kaufman for infusing me with Great Books and making me feel somehow equal to the task of writing this one. The members of Frontiers of Faith, for continuing to share their doubts, their wisdom and their life experiences with me. Father Luke Dysinger of St. Andrew's Abbey for his mind-altering thoughts on the Psalms. J. C. Wynkoop for rallying behind me in this and all endeavors. Our beloved Beach Avenue family who live in our hearts no matter here we go. And David Rusch for allowing me to work with his students. I can now tell my friend Rob that I am happiest when I am in a classroom full of budding teens attempting to turn their hearts into language.

I offer, too, a lifelong thanks to my mom for her unwavering desire to see her children speak the truth, whatever it might be, and regardless of whom it might offend.

As for the people who played the lead roles in this story, I hope that the preceding pages have said it best. This book is nothing if not a valentine to each of you.

I am blessed to spend my life in the company of three remarkable people for whom I thank God daily. My children, Graham and Remy, who ground me, inspire me and fill my days with purpose, anguish, awe, joy and love. And my husband, Lon, my hand to hold.